打開寶庫之門

Gateway to Infinite Dharma Treasure

by Sheng-yen Lu

A US Daden Culture Publication

US Daden Culture LLC
3440 Foothill Blvd.
Oakland, CA 94601
U.S.A.
Website: www.usdaden.com
Email: us.daden.culture@gmail.com

© 2018 by Sheng-yen Lu

The right of Living Buddha Lian-sheng, Sheng-yen Lu to be identified as author of this work including all translations based on his original writings, has been asserted by him in accordance with the Copyright, Designs, and Patents Act 1988.

All rights reserved. No part of this book may be reproduced in any form or by any means, electronic or mechanical, including photography, recording, or by any information storage or retrieval system or technologies now known or later developed, without permission in writing from the publisher.

Lu, Sheng-yen, 1945-
Gateway to Infinite Dharma Treasure by Sheng-yen Lu;
translated by Belinda Liu and Shizhong Duan;
edited by DJ Chang and Marc Streich;
proofread by Ronald Lee, DJ Chang, and Thomas W. Chung, Ph.D.

Library of Congress Control Number (PCN): 2018904923
ISBN-13: 978-0-9963807-5-1
ISBN-10: 0-9963807-5-2
1. True Buddha School. 2. Chinese-Tibetan Buddhism.
Cover design and layout by US Daden Culture Design Team
Photograph by US Daden Culture
Set in Minion Pro 12
US Daden books are printed on acid-free paper and meet the guidelines for the permanence and durability set by the Council of Library Resources.

Printed in the U.S.A.

Special Acknowledgements

The True Buddha Translation Teams (TBTTs) would like to express the highest honor and deepest gratitude to Living Buddha Lian-sheng Sheng-yen Lu and Master Lianxiang for their continuing support and guidance on the translation effort. Without their compassion, wisdom, blessings, and encouragement, this project would not have reached fruition.

In addition, we would like to acknowledge the diligent work put forth by the following volunteers: the leader of US Daden, Master Lianseng; Belinda Liu and Shizhong Duan (translators), DJ Chang and Marc Streich (editors), Ronald Lee and DJ Chang (proofreaders), and Thomas W. Chung, Ph.D. (proofreader and typesetter), and Renee Cordsen (typesetter and publication). We would like to thank these dedicated and selfless volunteers who have contributed their time and effort to promote the works of Living Buddha Lian-sheng, and to support the publications of US Daden Culture.

We would also like to extend our sincere appreciation to all of the other volunteers who work behind the scenes, facilitating the translation process, and handling administrative responsibilities.

May all volunteers be blessed with immeasurable merits. May all sentient beings benefit from the ocean of wisdom.

Table of Contents

Preface: Gateway to Infinite Dharma Treasure   1

1. Secret Key Formula is the Essence   5
2. The Ultimate Key Points   9
3. Stage of Insight and Cultivation of the Mind   13
4. Watching a Movie   17
5. Peace of Mind is Peace   21
6. Changes after Attaining Enlightenment   25
7. The Buddha-nature Appears Naturally   29
8. The Ultimate Wisdom   33
9. Forget Forget Forget Forget Forget   37
10. The Trilogy of Emptiness, Brightness and Bliss   41
11. Yoga Practice   45
12. Characteristics of Vajrayana Yogic Union   49
13. Secrets of Mahayoga   53
14. Invocation, Visualization and Mudra   57
15. Illusion within the Illusion   61
16. "Nothing Matters" Is the Key Point   65
17. The Fundamental Template of Vajrayana Cultivation   69

18. Benefits of Performing the Great Homage	73
19. The Secret of Changing from One Offering to Many	77
20. Opening the Door of Wisdom	81
21. Reciting the Vajrasattva Mantra	85
22. The Pure Heart of Bodhicitta	89
23. What Merits the Greatest Field of Blessings?	93
24. The Nature of Absolute Emptiness	97
25. The Leading Practices of the Vajrayana Completion Stage	101
26. Attaining Buddhahood through Qi Entering the Central Channel	105
27. Protection Practices (Part I)	109
28. Protection Practices (Part II)	113
29. Falling Asleep and Waking Up	117
30. Body Offering	121
31. A Stick of Burning Incense	125
32. Subtle Key Cultivation Formulas for Light Drops	129
33. To Achieve Peace of Mind	133
34. Key Points on Postures for Cultivating One's Body	137
35. Key Points on Empowerments	141
36. The Hum Syllable Purification Dharma (Speech Dharma)	145
37. Profound Insight of the Great Compassion Dharani (Speech Dharma)	149

38. Great Wisdom of Brightness and Emptiness (Cultivating one's Mind) 153
39. Eliminating the Habitual Tendencies of the Six Paths 157
40. The Key Formula for Awareness of Bright Light 161
41. The Light of Wisdom 165
42. Guard the Enlightenment Until It Is Solidified 169
43. Key Points for the Three Kinds of Emptiness 173
44. Key Formulas to Witness the Buddha-nature 177
45. The Ultimate Key Points of Sheng-yen Lu (Part 1) 181
46. The Ultimate Key Points of Sheng-yen Lu (Part 2) 185
47. The Ultimate Key Points of Sheng-yen Lu (Part 3) 189
48. The Ultimate Key Points of Sheng-yen Lu (Part 4) 193
49. The Ultimate Key Points of Sheng-yen Lu (Part 5) 197
50. A Letter from Master Lianhe 201

> Mind awakening is theoretical, a realization only in principle, whereas seeing the Buddha-nature is practical, realizing it by actual practices.
>
> Sheng-yen Lu

Preface: Gateway to Infinite Dharma Treasure

In this book, I want to tell everyone that I am the male protagonist in the book, and I am a treasure trove of dharma.
Why am I a treasure trove of dharma? The reasons are as follows:
Firstly:
I am gifted.
After my divine eye opened, I observed that I am actually the Padmakumara. I also journeyed to the Maha Twin Lotus Ponds, which is the Pure Land of the Padmakumara.
I composed this verse:
The original dharma body transcends the heavens.
An ancient pagoda and Buddhist relics however appeared;
Only for the sake of a great cause in the world of human beings,
Transformed into a monk and remained with sentient beings.
Who is Padmakumara? He is the Lotus-hand Bodhisattva, Xiangguang Youth, Baoyi Youth, Baoshang Youth, White Lotus King, White Maha Padmakumara...
He is the Lotus Light Unhindered Buddha.
Because of the above innate gift, I am a treasure trove of dharma.

Secondly:
I have attained spiritual union.

I have an affinity with cultivation, have practiced the Path of Accumulation, the Path of Preparation, the Path of Seeing, the True Path, and have practiced the Ultimate Path.

In Vajrayana Buddhism, I have practiced the Generation Stage perfectly.

In Vajrayana Buddhism, I have practiced the Completion Stage perfectly.

I have attained spiritual union in the Preliminary Practices, Guru Yoga, Principal Deity Yoga, Heruka Practices, Highest Yoga Tantra, and the Great Perfection.

In this life, I only engage myself in cultivation, writing, and disseminating the Buddhadharma.

I have attained spiritual union with Golden Mother of the Jade Pond, Amitabha Buddha, Ksitigarbha Bodhisattva and many more.

Because I am spiritually awakened, I am a treasure trove of dharma.

Thirdly:
I have awakened the mind.

The awakened mind is being enlightened. I understand that all the phenomenal realms should be viewed as an illusion, a bubble, a shadow, dew, or lightning. I understand the past mind, the present mind, and the future mind are all unobtainable. There is absolutely nothing to be attained.

I understand emptiness.

I understand nirvana.

I understand that "I alone am the honored one in the heavens and on earth."

After I awakened the mind, I realized the ultimate oneness, which is not two in opposition; it is absolute, not relative.

After awakening the mind, all my thoughts are calm, and everything is extinguished. Awakening is the totally empty and quiescent state which is constant and without discrimination.

The great wisdom is known by few people, so I am a treasure trove of dharma.

Fourthly:

I see the Buddha-nature.

Mind awakening is theoretical, a realization only in principle, whereas seeing the Buddha-nature is practical, realizing it by actual practices.

The Buddhist teachings are vast, and there are various schools. Each school and sect have their own respective practices. In Vajrayana Buddhism, the Great Perfection, Mahamudra, Yamantaka, and the Great Perfection Profound Wisdom are four great dharmas that I have practiced for forty years.

I have witnessed the Buddha-nature.

Witnessing the Buddha-nature is rare in the world, so I am a treasure trove of dharma.

Finally, what I want to tell everyone is:

Through my wisdom eye, the world, life, universe, cause and effect, reincarnation, nirvana, and everything are all an enormous illusion.

What I found is the ultimate of the Buddhadharma. Once reaching the ultimate, one will realize that even the Buddhadharma is not the Buddhadharma anymore. I have endless supernatural powers and subtle perceptions. Because of my wisdom, I have no regrets in my life!

If you read the book, you will also have a life without regrets.

All will praise this book!

Thumbs up!

Living Buddha Lian-sheng
Sheng-yen Lu
17102 NE 40th CT.
Redmond, WA, USA 98052

Sentient beings are in delusion; the enlightened being wants to wake up the ones in delusion.

Sheng-yen Lu

1. Secret Key Formula is the Essence

I would like to begin by telling a joke:
After turning in for the night, Mrs. Zhu chattered endlessly about some trivial household matters. Her husband however did not utter a word. After a while of jabbering, Mrs. Zhu stared at her husband and stated, "I have been talking all by myself. It is not fair. Now it's your turn to say something, and I'll listen." Mr. Zhu nodded and replied, "Good! I will speak now. It is late, so let's sleep!"

Ha ha ha!

I say:

What Mr. Zhu has said is the essence and a key formula. When it is time for bed, sleep!

This book does not contain long-winded theories. I will not use deep Buddhist terminology, nor will I lecture or preach. I just want to explain what I have achieved during my own practice, using the simplest language.

Remove branches and leaves.
Directly to the point.
Not talking much.

Only the essence.

For example:

A disciple asked, "Grand Master Lu came to the human world in this lifetime, what is the purpose?"

I replied, "To save sentient beings!"

The disciple asked, "What if someone does not believe you?"

I replied, "Continue to proclaim with a loud voice!"

The disciple asked, "What if someone already believes you?"

I replied, "Persist to proclaim with a loud voice!"

The disciple asked, "Why do you always proclaim with a loud voice?"

I replied, "Always continue to proclaim with a loud voice!"

The disciple asked, "Anything else?"

I replied, "No!"

Ha ha ha! I came to this world just to "announce with a loud voice," nothing else. That is the key formula.

The disciple asked, "Why does Grand Master Lu want to announce with a loud voice? Are you crazy?"

I replied, "I am an enlightened being who has awakened the mind and seen the Buddha-nature. Sentient beings are in delusion; the enlightened being wants to wake up the ones in delusion."

The disciple asked, "Are you crazy?"

I replied, "Yes, in the eyes of sentient beings, I'm a crazy dharma king, a crazy practitioner."

The disciple asked, "You claim you are enlightened, who can prove this?"

I replied, "No one can prove that I am enlightened, except the emptiness. I realized the emptiness; the emptiness has proven my realization. This is how "The dharma light will be turned on followed by the self-light being on."

I would like to tell everyone, my key formula:

"Emptiness."

It is simple.
It is clear.
It is pure.
It goes beyond name and form.
"Emptiness" is absolute, and not two in opposition.
"If you say existence?"
I'll reply, "Existence is also within the emptiness."
Emptiness and existence are both extinguished!

People with the wisdom eye see the instantaneous changes and understand that all things are illusory and unreal.

Sheng-yen Lu

2. The Ultimate Key Points

Let me start with a joke.
A person entered a noodle restaurant, and consumed a bowl of beef noodles, but found no beef with the noodles.

He asked the manager, "Manager! Manager! There is no beef in my beef noodles!"

The manager sarcastically replied, "When you eat a Sun Cake, does the Sun Cake have a sun in it?"

The guest was speechless.

Ha ha ha!

This joke has a profound meaning. "The Ultimate Key Points" appear within the joke.

I have often remarked:

The Sun Cake has no sun within.

The Moon Cake has no moon within.

The Wife Cake has no wife within.

(Recently, Taiwan has had a controversy over cooking oils. It has been discovered in Taiwan that olive oil has no olives, sesame oil has no sesames, peanut oil has no peanuts, and pepper oil has no pepper, etc.)

The key points are:

"Non-existence, non-existence, non-existence," that is "nothing, nothing, nothing," and is also "emptiness, emptiness, emptiness."

Thus, I often use the moon as an example. What is on the moon? There are no human beings, cars or houses on the moon. There is nothing on the moon. The moon has no privileges, no money, and no lust.

I ask:

On the moon, what is good? What is evil? What is right? What is wrong? What is the Buddha? What is Mara? What is happiness? What is anger? What is righteousness? What is wickedness? Etc.

I tell you, "Everything is a sea of clarity and serenity."

This is "no mind and no form."

The key points are:

Everyone believes that people and everything on the Earth truly exist because they seem so real.

But, we can think in such a way:

"People will die."

"Things will end."

"Objects will decay."

All tangible things on Earth cannot avoid the cycle of "formation, existence, decay, and disappearance." People with the wisdom eye see the instantaneous changes and understand that all things are illusory and unreal. If a practitioner can think in this manner, sooner or later they will be enlightened by the ultimate key point.

Remembering and practicing that thought is of foremost importance.

Remembering and practicing the key point, one can avoid distorted and deluded perceptions, far from greed, anger, ignorance, and afflictions.

Thus:

External phenomena become void and tranquil.
Emptying the mind within.
Be quiescent both internally and externally
How could the deluded mind arise?
Think about "the moon in the water," "the flower in the mirror," and yourself in the Saha world. What do you really obtain? By thinking this way, one will be thoroughly enlightened!

There is a poem in *Dream of the Red Chamber*. I shortened it as follows:

Mean hovels and abandoned halls,
Where courtiers once paid daily calls.
Bleak haunts where weeds and willows scarcely thrive,
Were once with mirth and revelry alive.

Would you of perfumed elegance recite?
Even as you speak, the raven locks turn white.
With fresh rouge and fragrant foundation,
The temple hair turns white.

Coffers with gold and silver filled,
Now...in a trice a tramp by all reviled.
One at some other's short life gives a sigh.
Not knowing that he too goes home - to die!
In such commotion does the world's theatre rage!
As each singer leaves, another takes the stage.
Most absurd.

The most important thing as a cultivator is being "single-minded."

Sheng-yen Lu

3. Stage of Insight and Cultivation of the Mind

Let me tell you a joke first!
A thin and weak lady by the name of Mrs. Hsu was re-elected President of the Women's Association. When she came on stage to give a speech, she humorously said, "I have been elected President of the association consecutively a few times. When everyone sees me, they shout President, President [same pronunciation in Chinese as being able to grow taller]. However, in fact, I'm still short. I am not growing any taller."

Ha ha ha!

I can honestly tell you, if you are a person with an enlightened mind, you must surely know:

Neither increasing nor decreasing.
Neither impurity nor purity.
Neither coming nor going.
Neither taking nor giving.

The Buddha-nature is primordial and constant. It does not grow!

We cultivators must first have this stage of insight, and this insight is the key point.

I will tell a second joke!

A wife said, "There was a man who was sentenced to one year in prison, because he married two wives."

The husband replied, "He's so lucky! I just married one wife, but was sentenced to a lifetime of imprisonment."

Ha ha ha!

I tell you, this is a joke about being "single-minded."

The most important thing as a cultivator is being "single-minded."

First become aware of the Buddha-nature.

Then we must keep in mind and constantly practice, also known as maintaining one's practice after awakening. This is "single-minded," and being "single-minded" is very important.

Cognition of the Buddha-nature, keeping the cognition in mind, and practicing single-mindedly and constantly are the skills and key formula for mind cultivation.

Cognition is the principle.

Keeping in mind and practicing continuously is to realize the principle.

Just understanding the Buddha-nature is of no use if the understanding is only in principle. You must always keep in mind, never forget, maintain and practice the principle. This is the effort of actually realizing the cognition.

Let me give you an example:

A lamp is only external in appearance.

It needs to be connected to an electrical source in order to emit light.

The electrical connection must be single-minded. (The electricity must remain on.)

After having gained this stage of insight, you must go to cultivate the mind. Having gained this stage of insight can only be considered teaching, but does not benefit cultivating the mind at all. Cultivating the mind is practice.

One Zen master said:
Enlightenment is like riding a bull.
Cultivation of the mind is like controlling the bull and not trampling on the garden.
Therefore, developing bodhicitta and not hurting people are very important key points.
Do not hurt people!
But help people instead!
This is the key point of being a bodhisattva.
I sincerely tell all of you:
At the beginning of studying Buddhism -
The goal is to attain the awareness of the Buddha-nature.
At the end of studying Buddhism -
The goal is to manifest the Buddha-nature.
This is the stage of insight and cultivating the mind.
Keeping in mind and practicing continuously are the unsurpassed key points.
Do you want to be free?
Do you want to be happy?
Do you want to be unrestrained?
Then you must go to find a master who is truly enlightened and can teach one the utmost important key points.
Who is the most worthy enlightened master?
He is right in front of you.

Where there is life, there must be death. This is the immutable, universal truth.

Sheng-yen Lu

4. Watching a Movie

One day, we went to watch a movie, it was "The Hobbit." Some of the characters in the movie included: Hobbits, Orcs, Elf people, and an evil dragon.

The movie began with a king at the foot of a mountain who tried to regain their ancestral power, gold, silver, and jewelry.

This movie has no beginning or end. In the movie, if you do not connect the story with "The Lord of the Rings," then essentially there is no beginning and no ending.

The fighting in the movie was exciting.

Our minds were captivated by the thrilling fight scenes.

Only at the conclusion of the movie, could we breathe a sigh of relief. Whew! Moreover, I was I and the movie was the movie.

The conclusion:

"We just watched a movie!"

Therefore, "Life is merely a drama playing out." This is the key point I want to impart to everyone.

A practitioner should observe the drama as a bystander. No matter what happens in the drama, one should constantly remain a bystander.

When one reviews one's own life from birth to death, is it not a drama? One must awaken from this drama.

By always observing as a bystander, one will attain realization.

One laughs out loud and realizes this is how it is. This is how it is. Life is like watching and acting in a movie.

When the drama ends, one should be enlightened! Isn't your body and mind free now?

We best be "bystanders." One acting in this manner is a sensible person.

Even if you are the main character, you should understand that life is just a drama. As a result, your body and mind are liberated.

Here is a joke:

Mr. and Mrs. Lu went shopping. After coming back, Mrs. Lu happily said, "Earlier on the road, lots of men looked at me!"

Mr. Lu replied coldly, "Let them look! Otherwise, as soon as you come home, no one at all will look at you!"

Ha ha ha!

From this joke, what can you sense?

When you are alive, you act and watch.

Upon your death, the drama ends.

No one can avoid death. Fame, status, power and beauty all change ownership at the moment of death. Where there is life, there must be death. This is the immutable, universal truth.

You're an actor.

You are also a bystander.

Hey brother!

Take it easy! Why so nervous?

In this world, what's the big deal?

It's just a drama!

The key point of my article is "life is a drama." Only in this way, can one be in an "unoccupied" mood, be of "no-thought" attitude, and enter the "single-minded" Samadhi (meditation).

If you are still:
Ignorant.
Afflicted.
Scatterbrained.
Stubborn.
Struggling.
Ugh! What else can I say?

The three sentences are drawn from the truths realized by Shakyamuni Buddha, which are impermanence, no self, nirvana, and quiescence.

Sheng-yen Lu

5. Peace of Mind is Peace

Recently I often walk by Shizheng Road in Taichung, Taiwan. While walking by, I noticed a large banner that read "Peace of mind - Peace" hung high on a building under construction.

The banner reminded me of the six characters in the airport's VIP lounge written by the Venerable Master Sheng Yen:

"Peace of Mind Is Peace."[In Chinese, the phrase has six characters]

I laughed out loud after reading the banner!

In fact, Master Sheng Yen's slogan "Peace of Mind Is Peace" is not wrong. It is right.

However, he forgot that one's mind is restless as long as one is a human being. Everyone has afflictions. How can one achieve peace of mind?

Let me provide two jokes as examples.

The first joke is:

Old Mr. Wang congratulated young Mr. Li, "Congratulations to both of you. True love always results in marriage. Your love finally produced results."

Mr. Li said with a wry smile, "Yikes! We have been married for only three months and my wife is already pregnant. It seems lovers eventually become a tired couple."

The second joke is:

A patient told the doctor, "I'm very upset. I obviously have amnesia. What can I do?"

The doctor said, "Go home! You just need to forget about it. Then, your illness will be healed!"

Ha ha ha!

I knowingly smile at these two jokes. Although jokes, they contain hidden truths. This proves that afflictions are everywhere.

Having "peace of mind" is not easy for people!

I have a key point here which I have said before and repeat it often:

First, everyone will die.

Second, everything will fade away.

Third, all matter will decay.

I often think of these three sentences. By thinking of these three sentences, one will have peace of mind.

Therefore, these three sentences are the key points for attaining peace of mind.

In my life, I have encountered numerous people, events, and things. One wave after another arises endlessly...

Thinking of the key points of these three sentences keeps my mind peaceful!

Thus:

Peace of mind - Peace.

Peace of mind is peace.

This is Master Sheng Yen's slogan.

However, I only use the key points. People will die, everything will fade away, and all matter will decay. As a result, the mind will naturally become peaceful.

Having people shout slogans is not enough; you have to teach sentient beings how to make their minds peaceful!

Perhaps you do not know the source of these three sentences. The three sentences are drawn from the truths realized by Shakyamuni Buddha, which are impermanence, no self, nirvana, and quiescence.

Someone said, "What Grand Master Lu spoke is Nihilism!"

I replied, "No, it is not!"

I keep my body and mind unhindered (peace of mind) and free from attachment. With this attitude, I do my best to handle people and matters. I make great effort to spread the Buddhadharma and to cultivate. This is bodhi and compassion. However, I do not care about the outcome. This is the ultimate wisdom of Buddha's teaching.

I understand this, so I have no afflictions and nothing matters!

Although you already know nothing is to be attained, can you still "transcend" the temptations?

Sheng-yen Lu

6. Changes after Attaining Enlightenment

I'll tell you three jokes first:
A wife looking in a mirror angrily stated, "It seems I am getting older and older, and getting uglier and uglier."

Her husband responded coldly, "You seem to have a knack for the obvious."

(Changes due to the passage of time.)

Also:

A said to B, "My wife often says that marriage can change a man, make him grow, and learn a lot of things."

B agreed, "She is right. After marriage, I learned to do laundry, grocery shopping, cooking, and housework."

(Changes after being married.)

Also:

A wife asked her husband, "Before marriage, when you and I met, you always said that your heart was beating like a 'blindly-running deer.' Do you still have this feeling?"

The husband replied, "Not anymore!"

"Why?" His wife asked.

The husband answered, "The deer already crashed into something and died a long time ago!"

Ha ha ha!

I use these three jokes as examples to emphasize "changes." However, after attaining enlightenment, will a practitioner truly gain strength to alter their habits and afflictions?

We often say, "Mountains can be moved, but one's nature is hard to change."

"People's habits are deeply rooted, and to change a person's stubborn nature is not easy."

I often say that water can extinguish a fire. However, when a fire is large and the water supply is low, it is like trying to put out a burning pile of wood with a cup of water. How can one do it?

Although fire can boil water, if there is only a little flame, how long will it take to boil a full bathtub of water?

By the same token, when one has just attained enlightenment, how can one free oneself from the entanglement of "money, power, fame, status, love and enjoyment" while one still has karmic hindrances, habits, affinities, the seven human emotions, and six desires accumulated over lifetimes.

That is why there is "cultivation after enlightenment."

However, whether you can succeed or not all depends on whether you have enough power of concentration and wisdom. (Many enlightened practitioners still have greed, anger, ignorance, doubts and arrogance.)

Everyone knows:

Everyone will die.

Everything will fade away.

All objects will decay.

However, when the temptations arrive, are you able to "instantaneously cease" them? Although you already know nothing is to be attained, can you still "transcend" the temptations?

This is why "cultivation starts after enlightenment!"
You have to achieve the following:
To reach the other shore.
To liberate oneself from the entanglement of afflictions and habits.
To end secular life, transcend the secular world, and be enlightened.
This indeed is not easy, so the key point I use is "perseverance."

"Perseverance" is necessary in one's whole life. Myriad practices subsumed in the six perfections are inseparable from "perseverance."

I have many disciples who have "awakened their minds," but still a lot of them show worldly attachments. It is very difficult to transcend the six paths of reincarnation. I advise all holy disciples to exercise "perseverance," "Instantaneous cessation" and "Instantaneously transcend" all temptations. Only then can one's Buddha-nature appear naturally.

One must be able to be "instantaneously enlightened."

Also one must be able to "cultivate gradually."

As long as there is no nagging, the pure Buddha-nature will show up naturally!

Sheng-yen Lu

7. The Buddha-nature Appears Naturally

Someone asked me, "How do you witness the Buddha-nature?" I replied, "Naturally."

I was asked again, "Why is it natural? Doesn't one discover Buddha-nature through perseverance?"

I replied, "No! As long as one removes deluded thoughts, the Buddha-nature is right there."

I emphasize:

The Buddha-nature always exists.

The Buddha-nature is immaculate and bright.

The Buddha-nature does not depend on cultivation.

One does not cultivate Buddha-nature. The Buddha-nature will appear naturally as long as one cultivates with perseverance and achieves no mind.

To state the point more clearly:

As clouds disperse and water flows away, heaven and earth become silent and empty.

With people and cows all disappearing, that is the moment of the bright moon.

The most important key point is:

"Do not be occupied with seeing the Buddha-nature. One just ceases the deluded thoughts."

I will tell you two jokes:

A wife asked, "What do you think about monogamy?"

The husband replied, "I agree with half."

The wife asked, "Why do you say that?"

The husband replied, "I am in favor of one husband, against one wife."

(Ha ha ha! I also agree with half. One only needs to remove deluded thoughts without seeking the truth, because once the deluded thoughts are evaporated, the truth appears naturally.)

The second joke:

A asked B, "Don't you have a new sports car? Why do you still drive that worn-out car each time when traveling with your wife?"

B answered, "Ah! Only the cacophony of that aged car can drown out the nagging of my wife."

Ha ha ha!

As long as there is no nagging, the pure Buddha-nature will show up naturally!

I say:

In the *Heart Sutra*, it says, "Liberating oneself from illusion is the absolute nirvana."

To liberate oneself from illusion, one must not attach to:

1. The illusory human world - thinking that this unreal world truly exists and will be eternal.
2. The worldly pleasures - thinking that worldly pleasure is the goal to chase. Consider wealth, beauty, fame, food and sleep are fundamental to a happy life and therefore tightly attach to them.
3. Discrimination - all day long, one compares and differentiates between righteousness and evil, good and bad, right and wrong, beauty and ugliness, positive and negative, separateness and

togetherness, etc., living in a state of two opposing elements without ceasing deluded thoughts.
4. Self-centeredness - treating the "self" as the center; one considers that "I" truly exists. The physical body of one proves that "I" am actual. The mind of everything serving me causes all kinds of distorted delusive thoughts.

The key points of cultivation are:
1. The world is a delusion.
2. There is no sadness and happiness.
3. The true suchness is absolute.
4. "I" is no-self.

I am a sensible person. All disciples must firmly keep these key points in mind as well as realizing them diligently with perseverance, which will save not only oneself but also others.

Liberation and bodhi fall within these parameters.

If someone says the Buddha has discoursed on the dharma, then that is slandering the Buddha.

Sheng-yen Lu

8. The Ultimate Wisdom

I would like to tell a joke first:
A man said, "My wife and I almost argue and fight every day. After a fierce quarrel last week, we have had a full week without quarrelling, and this week is quite pleasant."

His friend asked, "Have you reconciled together already?"

The man replied, "Back together? How is that possible! She ran away from home, and to this day has not returned!"

Ha ha ha!

Why did I tell this joke? I used the wife as an analogy for "afflictions." People always live with "afflictions," entanglements with no end.

Until "afflictions" are eliminated, one is unable to live a pleasant life.

If "afflictions" never return, that is what is known as "purity."

Let's proceed to the main topic.

What was Shakyamuni Buddha's enlightened revelation under the bodhi tree? My understanding is that he was enlightened about "Tathagata."

"Tathagata" originally means "Thus Come One."

The word "Tathagata" is very significant.
One seems to come.
One seems not to come.
One seems to exist and yet one seems not to exist.
One seems to be and yet one seems not to be.
I often use an analogy of the "moon in the water."
In the night sky, there is a large and round moon above. When the moon reflects on a calm lake, it appears in the lake as well.
(Water is in a thousand rivers, so is a moon in a thousand rivers.)
Does the moon in the water exist?
It looks like it exists by what we have seen with our eyes.
Does the moon in the water not exist?
It does not exist when you try to scoop it up.
I would like to point out the ultimate wisdom is exactly like this.
Shakyamuni Buddha said the following:
"Although having expounded the dharma for forty-nine years, I have never said a single word.
If someone says the Buddha has discoursed on the dharma, then that is slandering the Buddha.
Perceiving phenomena but realizing it is not phenomena, then one sees the Tathagata.
All phenomena are unreal and false.
Nothing to be gained.
Nothing to be said.
The so-called Buddhadharma is not the Buddhadharma.
The mind should stay in a non-abiding state.
No mark of self, no mark of people, no mark of sentient beings, no mark of having a life span.
All the differentiating characteristics of things are non-phenomena; all sentient beings are not sentient beings.
Bodhisattvas who understand the dharma of selflessness are considered by buddhas to be true bodhisattvas.

All conditioned dharmas are like an illusion, a bubble, a shadow, dew, or lightning, and should be viewed as such."
I will tell everyone and all holy disciples:
This is the ultimate wisdom.
I say:
Wisdom accomplishes Buddhahood,
Otherwise one becomes an evil demon;
Good and evil are all karma,
By which the Six Realms are generated.

What I have said should be clear enough. It cannot be stated more explicitly. I like the word "Tathagata" the most. One seems to come, and one seems not to come. If people can understand these words, becoming enlightened will not be a problem. "Tathagata" is the key point that I, Grand Master Lu, employ.

With the key point of "Tathagata" in mind while reading the *Diamond Sutra*, one will comprehend the entire sutra clearly.

Although the "mind" and "phenomena" both exist, one should not attach to either the "mind" or "phenomena."

Sheng-yen Lu

9. Forget Forget Forget Forget Forget

The key moment in Shakyamuni Buddha's life occurred during the period he sat under the bodhi tree at Bodh Gaya. Facing east, sitting cross-legged in a full-lotus position, he vowed never to rise if he did not attain enlightenment.

Later, at dawn, the Buddha realized that he had already eliminated all afflictions and any taint of earthly attachments. He awakened the mind and saw the Buddha-nature. Thus, he transcended the Six Paths of Reincarnation and attained the unexcelled state of Perfect Enlightenment.

The Buddha's initial turning of the Dharma wheel was represented through T*he Discourse on the Establishing of Mindfulness* [*Satipatthana Sutra*]. The key points:

Realize suffering.
Sever the mind from suffering.
Be enlightened about the extinguishment of suffering.
Cultivate the enlightenment.

The Buddha's second turning of the Dharma wheel was represented through the *Large Perfection of Wisdom Sutra* [*Mahaprajnaparamita*

Sutras]. The key points:
Attain enlightenment and awaken the mind.
Prajna wisdom.
Myriad practices subsumed in the six perfections.

The Buddha's third turning of the Dharma wheel was represented through the *Sutra on Understanding Profound and Esoteric Doctrine* [*Sandhinirmocana Sutra*]. The key topics:
The Consciousness-only.
The Middle Way.
Yoga.
Vajrayana.

Theravada Buddhism believes the Buddha cultivated bodhisattva practices in countless past lived, and accumulated the two necessary provisions for the path to enlightenment. Until descending, being reborn, and attaining enlightenment in the Saha World, he then truly became the Buddha in Bodh Gaya.

However, Mahayana Buddhism believes that Buddha had long ago attained enlightenment in the past. The reason he descended and was reborn in the world of human beings was only a "play." His purpose of the manifestation was to demonstrate to sentient beings that ordinary beings can also achieve perfect enlightenment.

Personally, I believe:

"Play" is the key cultivation formula. If a cultivator watches sentient beings with a "playing" mind and subsequently looks back upon themselves, the practitioner will not then attach to people, matters, and objects.

Non-attachment is namely "Forget, forget, forget, forget, forget ..."

Although the "mind" and "phenomena" both exist, one should not attach to either the "mind" or "phenomena."

Be natural.

Forget everything and be affliction free.

Here is a story that will highlight the key point:

A youth walked into an art exhibition room. The youth perambulated in a big circle, perusing the world famous paintings. After viewing all the paintings, he totally forgot everything.

This is called "Youth viewing paintings."

Although the youth did view all the paintings, not even one image of the paintings remained in the youngster's mind.

This is a "play," and also forgetting.

If practitioners watch themselves and the surrounding environment with a "playing" mind, forgetting everything with nothing in the mind, then nothing can affect the practitioners' mind. As a result, the practitioners will have no emotional fluctuations and rising of their delusive thoughts.

Buddha's playing in the Saha world is the same as "Playing Lion Buddha." Once the "play" ends, everything is forgotten.

"Play" is the key point.

Forgetting is also the key point.

Here is a joke:

What is the difference between Valentine's Day and Tomb Sweeping Day?

The answer is:

On both Valentine's Day and Tomb Sweeping Day, we send flowers.

However, on Valentine's Day, we spend real money to buy flowers, and say a bunch of boldface lies to the lover; whereas during Tomb Sweeping Day, we burn fake money, and tell the truth to the ghosts.

Ha ha ha!

Everything is a "play"; do not let anything attach to your mind; forget about everything.

To "not forget" is the way of the ordinary people!

To "forget" is the way of a wise sage!

With equality and a true nature, dharma body is also devoid of discrimination.

Sheng-yen Lu

10. The Trilogy of Emptiness, Brightness and Bliss

I often mention that the differences among the Three Realms are:
Emptiness - corresponds to the Formless Realm.
Brightness - corresponds to the Form Realm.
Bliss - corresponds to the Desire Heavens.

This "Emptiness" refers to the emptiness of the Four Heavens also known as the Caturupabrahmaloka Heavens. "Brightness" refers to the adornment of brightness, and "Bliss" refers to incomparable happiness.

To reach emptiness, brightness and bliss, one needs to practice step by step.

Someone asked me, "Are emptiness, brightness and bliss associated with buddha's dharma body, reward body and emanation body?"

I replied, "There are similarities and differences!"

I explained that the buddha's three bodies are as follows:

Dharma Body - This is the essence of all phenomena. Dharma body is also known as true suchness, emptiness, truth, reality, true mind, etc. It is very difficult to explain.

Therefore, dharma body constantly exists. It is not judgemental, created, extinguished, dirty, clean, coming, going, identical, different, or distinct. With equality and a true nature, dharma body is also devoid of discrimination. The body, the mind, the dharma, and the nature of the dharma body are all empty.

We often say that the "dharma-body buddha" is Mahavairocana Buddha, the Great Sun Tathagata.

(This emptiness of the dharma body transcends the Four Formless Heavens.)

Reward Body - This is a perfectly complete physical body rewarded for a buddha who has full merits. The body has the 32 major marks and 80 minor marks. It is an illusory transformation of endless light without a self-nature. Vairocana Buddha is a reward-body buddha.

All buddhas that manifest in the pure lands are reward-body buddhas. Shakyamuni Buddha's reward body resides in the Akanistha Heaven.

(The light of a buddha's reward body is brighter and more endless than the light of the Heaven of Form.)

Emanation Body – emanated in the world for the purpose of saving sentient beings of the Six Paths due to compassion towards them.

The reason for an emanation body manifesting in the world is to serve as an enlightened teacher who is commissioned to save sentient beings with indiscriminate compassion.

Emanation-body buddhas (also known as transformation-body buddhas) emerge to guide and benefit sentient beings.

As long as the world continues to exist and reincarnation does not cease, so will the transformation-body buddhas continue to appear.

Emanation-body buddhas teach sentient beings to cultivate.

They have different forms and are omnipresent.

In the human world, Shakyamuni Buddha is an emanation-body buddha.

I understand that:

Emptiness – corresponds to the dharma body.
Brightness – corresponds to the reward body.
The awareness of brightness – corresponds to the emanation body (or transformation body.)
Simply put in this way:
"Emptiness, brightness, emptiness brightness together."
Emptiness leads to the achievement of the dharma-body buddha.
Adornment of brightness leads to the achievement of the reward-body buddha.
The awareness of brightness leads to the achievement of the emanation-body buddha (or transformation-body buddha).
I have spoken so much, but in the end what is the key point?
The key point is only one word:
"Practice."
There is a joke:
A man said, "My wife recently has become obsessed with playing the harmonica, I love it!"
His friend asked, "Why?"
The man answered, "She practices the harmonica every day, so she won't have time to nag me!"
Ha ha ha!
There are benefits for everyone through my teaching practice:
By practicing, one attains enlightenment followed by terminating the greedy mind, delusive thoughts, afflictions, and confusions. One then becomes purified and unpolluted. The word "practice" is the starting point for sentient beings to achieve liberation.
There is only one word for one who desires liberation from the Six Paths of Reincarnation:
"Practice."

It is like one's breath, heart-beat, and mind are connected to one's personal deity that comes from the depths of your soul.

Sheng-yen Lu

11. Yoga Practice

I would like to tell a joke:
A renowned fortune teller was invited to foresee a newborn's fate.

The fortune teller stated, "This child has an auspicious face, and the fortune of an emperor. When he matures, he will have cars provided to him for transportation, live in luxurious hotels, enjoy the supportive company of people everywhere, visit famous attractions and historical sites, and enjoy endless food and drink. No matter where he journeys, there will be a group of people closely following him..."

"Wow! That sounds so great!"

Later, when the person grew up, he became a tourist guide.

Ha ha ha! The fortune teller was correct!

I have said that in the Vajrayana development stage, there are methods of "spiritual union." What is spiritual union? It is yoga.

Spiritual union is the following:

To be one.

Spiritual resonance.

Interconnected.

Perfectly complete.

We Vajrayana practitioners practice the "Four Preliminary Practices Spiritual Union," "Guru Yoga," "Deity Yoga" and so on.

A poetic verse from a poem by Li Shangyin states:
The body does not have colorful phoenix's wings,
With a hint the mind can reach tacit understanding.

Spiritual union is really wonderful and very mysterious. It is unification of mind with mind; that is, two become one.

Sleep together every night.

Get up together every morning.

A phenomenon of reliance on each other.

It is like one's breath, heart-beat, and mind are connected to one's personal deity that comes from the depths of your soul. Bit by bit, one can clearly understand one's personal deity's intention, accurately and with no errors.

Completely unified!

Your personal deity is within your mind.

You are within your personal deity's mind.

I repeat this often. Whenever I'm on a plane and the moment I sit down, I recite the mantra of my personal deity. I visualize my personal deity until my personal deity is atop my head, entering my heart, and becoming one with me.

At this moment, there is nothing to worry about!

No matter what happens, I will journey to my personal deity's Pure Land, because I have fully unified with my personal deity.

I would like to tell everyone:

Vajrayana practitioners should always remember their own personal deity, the root guru, or the root dharma protector. They should do this all of the time.

Cultivate yoga practice.

Visualize one's personal deity.

Chant the mantra of one's personal deity.

Form the mudra of one's personal deity.

I have the most important key point for practitioners to attain spiritual union with one's personal deity. The key point is that one should at least consume some of the offerings one makes to one's personal deity. It is the best if one is able to eat all without giving any to others.

Another important point is that one makes the identical vows as to the personal deity's. Do not differentiate one's vows from the personal deity's. One should also have the identical vows in each cultivation.

Eat the same food. (Body transformation)

Have the same vows. (Mind transformation)

These are the most important key points of the Principal Deity Yoga!

Now, one can achieve Buddhahood within one lifetime.

Sheng-yen Lu

12. Characteristics of Vajrayana Yogic Union

We Buddhists all know that gradual cultivation takes "three incalculable eons" to attain Buddhahood.
One first practices:
Generosity, precepts, patience, diligence, meditation and wisdom.
Then, one perceives:
Emptiness of person.
Emptiness of phenomena.
Emptiness of no-self.
Emptiness.
Furthermore, one eliminates afflictions and habitual tendencies.
With gradual cultivation, one experiences the "path of accumulation," the "path of applied practices," the "path of insight," the "path of cultivation," and the "ultimate path."
This is the cultivation method of the Mahayana and the "Bodhisattva Vehicle."
Since:
Vajrayana Buddhism is a branch of Mahayana Buddhism, therefore Vajrayana Buddhism naturally follows this sequence. However,

Vajrayana Buddhism has a unique expedient practice, which is "yogic union" that does not exist in Sutrayana Buddhism. Yogic union practice is a characteristic of Vajrayana Buddhism.

We call the practice "Celestial Yoga," also known as "Personal Deity Yoga."

In this special practice, the practitioner selects a personal deity. By visualizing, forming the mudra, and reciting the mantra, one unites oneself with the personal deity.

The personal deity may be a buddha or a bodhisattva who appears in a divine form. Then, the practitioner closely connects or even unites as one with the divine form materializing for expediency. As a result, the practitioner radiates "divine pride."

What I mean is that the practice of unifying with one's personal deity is a method that does not exist in other sects. This is the distinguishing feature of Vajrayana Buddhism.

When I spiritually unify with Golden Mother of the Jade Pond, I am Golden Mother of the Jade Pond.

When I spiritually unify with Amitabha, I am Amitabha.

When I spiritually unify with Ksitigarbha Bodhisattva, I am Ksitigarbha Bodhisattva.

This is taking "Fruition" as the "Path."

We also believe that the Vajrayana yogic union practice can reduce the cultivation time. Originally, one has to go through the "three incalculable eons." Now, one can achieve Buddhahood within one lifetime.

The practice is "expediency" and "swiftly accomplishing."

The common points of Mahayana are:

"To benefit all sentient beings in achieving Buddhahood together."

"All dharma has empty self-nature."

However, the most prominent feature of Vajrayana is the "Celestial Personal Deity Yoga" which is the integration of Vajrayana Buddhism's unique "expediency" and "wisdom."

In other Mahayana Buddhist schools, the practitioner and wisdom accompany and assist each other.

However, in Vajrayana Buddhism, the practitioner and wisdom unite as one.

Only through such an expedient method of visualizing the union of one with one's personal deity can a practitioner accomplish sufficient merits to initiate the uncommon practices of unification of the reward body and the emanation body.

I regard this "subtle key point."

Vajrayana Buddhism itself is already the "key point."

Personally, I began as a Christian, became a Taoist, practiced Sutrayana Buddhism, and then cultivated Vajrayana. Since then I have focused on practicing Vajrayana Buddhism because I have appreciated the method of unifying with one's personal deity.

Here is a short joke:

What does a bachelor's residence look like?

All the houseplants are dead

But plant mold grows in the refrigerator

I tell you:

Surrounding me and within me are buddhas and bodhisattvas!

The original meaning of practice is transformation and purification.

Sheng-yen Lu

13. Secrets of Mahayoga

Upon achieving union in my "Personal Deity Yoga," I naturally understand the original meaning of "divine pride."

It turns out that "divine pride" is Mahayoga.

When one becomes the personal deity, one can enter Mahayoga.

Food -- purified then transforms into nectar.

Clothing -- purified then transforms into subtle celestial garments.

Dwelling -- purified then transforms into the personal deity's palace.

Walking -- purified then transforms into the personal deity's undertakings.

Education -- purified then transforms into the personal deity's divine pride.

Happiness -- purified then transforms into the personal deity's entertainment.

Human beings -- purified then transform into the personal deity's retinue of heavenly beings.

Sound -- purified then transforms into mantra.

Etc...

In fact, these are collectively named "divine pride," which is the visualization of a practitioner mirroring the personal deity.

Actions simulating the personal deity are likely to be interpreted by the outside world as:

Self-deception.

Arrogance.

Meaninglessness.

However, I personally believe that, through this process, one is already practicing. Mahayoga itself is practice. The original meaning of practice is transformation and purification. Is it not so?

While walking the path of cultivation, the secular people need to transform and purify all of their original five aggregates, concepts, and desires.

Moreover, everything in the world is without a self-nature. We practitioners use "visualization," "mudra," and "mantra" to transform and purify all worldly things to that of the personal deity's.

Even more brilliant is:

Five afflictions (five aggregates) - transformed into the Five Wisdom Buddhas.

Desire - transformed into the Buddha Mother.

Wealth, lust, fame, food and sleep - transformed into the bodhisattva.

Anger - transformed into the vajra protector.

What I want to stress is that all dharmas are guided by the mind; therefore "purification and transformation" are the key points.

Cultivation is a part of it.

Even the "Consort Practice" is purification and transformation too.

Unification of secular men and women is "sexual lust."

All ordinary people are subject to sexual gratification as it is a common thing. However, if purified and transformed, mundane unification becomes a cultivation.

In regard to the Consort Practice, there is too much criticism and abuse, which creates difficulty in providing a clear explanation.

However, in Mahayoga, it is nothing more than purification and transformation of the sexual lust between secular men and women or between lay practitioners.

(The fear is that human beings who are enamoured with lust may use the name of the Consort Practice to engage in deception and adultery.)

Now, everyone should understand that my key points are "purification and transformation."

I would like to tell two jokes:

Mr. Wang entered into his wife's room smiling and said, "The children are clamoring to see the tiger at the zoo."

Mrs. Wang was furious, "It is raining so heavily, how can we go out?"

Mr. Wang said, "Right! Can you please do me a favor and move to the living room, so that the children can take a look at you!"

Ha ha ha! This is the transformation!

Here is my second joke:

One day, someone asked Mr. Wang, "While attending a burial ceremony, should I walk in front of the hearse or behind?"

Mr. Wang replied, "As long as you don't sleep inside the coffin, you can walk where you please!"

Ha ha ha!

Transformation results in freedom and non-hinderance.

In silence, one enters the samadhi.

Sheng-yen Lu

14. Invocation, Visualization and Mudra

I would like to tell a joke first:
A man said, "My wife insists on meditation before going to bed, it really bothers me!"
His friend asked, "Does she speak during meditation?"
The man replied, "No! She sits less than three minutes, and starts snoring like thunder!"
Here is another joke:
A woman said to her husband, "A moment ago, that beggar we saw around the corner looked awful, was he sick?"
Her husband replied, "No, it was because you only threw a dollar to him!"
(Ha ha ha!)
The reason I mentioned these two jokes is mainly because they relate to the main topic.
There are key points in practicing invocation, visualization, mantra recitation, and mudra formation of one's personal deity. The novice practitioners must pay attention to them.
Let's begin with the three-stage visualization.
One first empties the mind. Visualize a moon disc appearing.

Inside the moon disc is a seed syllable. The seed syllable emits light and the personal deity appears.

The key cultivation formulas to invoke one's personal deity are explained with the following examples:

If one is to invoke Avalokitesvara, one visualizes her celestial garments floating and fluttering in the air. When focusing more deeply, one visualizes her jade-pearl necklace and bracelets slightly moving. These are the key points.

If one is to invoke Manjushri Bodhisattva, one visualizes the sword in his hand, moving and swinging.

If one is to invoke Vajrapani Bodhisattva or other Dharma protectors, one visualizes lightning bolts and the sound of thunder, "Hum Hum."

These are the key points.

In terms of reciting mantras:

For purification – use a soft sound. (Compassionate)

For enhancement - use an eager sound. (Powerful and urgent)

For subjugation - use a stern sound. (Roaring)

For harmonization - use a happy sound. (Joyful)

In terms of forming the mudras:

For purification – softly hold the mudra.

For enhancement – firmly hold the mudra.

For subjugation – swing the mudra.

For harmonization – gently rub the mudra.

The mudra is and needs to touch the heart of the personal deity. There are other secret mudra formulas that I will not discuss here, because there are too many personal deities for me to list their individual formulas.

In terms of colors:

White - for purification.

Yellow - for enhancement.

Blue - for subjugation.

Red - for harmonization.

These formulas are applied widely and with versatility to the "form yoga" within the Action and Performance Tantras.

However, the formulas are applied less in the Yoga Tantra and Highest Yoga Tantra, mainly because the tantras are the "formless yoga."

For example, if reciting mantra before entering samadhi, one will recite the mantra silently. One then visualizes a seed syllable appearing in the fire of one's body and mind and emitting light. In silence, one enters the samadhi.

I think Vajrayana is very vibrant. For example, there are four analogies used in "merging of self and deity," in which the personal deity enters into the heart of the practitioner. The four tantras also employ such analogies.

Looking at each other – the practitioner and the personal deity look at each other.

Smiling - the practitioner and the personal deity like each other.

Embracing - the practitioner and the personal deity become intimate with each other.

Unifying – Two sexual organs unite.

The appearance of a father-mother buddha in Vajrayana is simply to symbolize the unification of expediency and wisdom. It is a phenomenon of spiritual union and two merging into one, a representation of perfection.

No need to be shocked and mortified.

This is a nexus of the worldly and supramundane.

The fruition of Buddhahood is equal, deep, permanent, unique, wonderful, pure, bright, and with perfect enjoyment.

Sheng-yen Lu

15. Illusion within the Illusion

Let me tell you two jokes first:
A woman asked, "Your boyfriend is great! He is tall, handsome, and also an authoritative cardiologist. How can you break up with him?"
Her friend replied, "What's the use, he never listens to my heartfelt wishes!"
Ha ha ha!
In addition:
A woman listened to her friend explaining the process of her getting ill. The friend explained the illness in great detail, and was most serious.
However, while listening at great length, the woman dozed off.
Suddenly she woke up and asked her friend, "So did you die?"
Ha ha ha!
There are illusions in both jokes.
Many people are curious about the illusory body in Vajrayana. What actually is the illusory body?
Many people have asked me, "What is the illusory body?"

"The illusory body is unreal." I replied.

However, everyone will understand the illusory body clearly when we use the term "soul" in ordinary people's language.

The soul is essentially the "bardo."

However, the souls have different levels:

Ghosts. (Lesser power)

Gods. (Greater power)

Nature spirits. (Ability to change)

Buddhas. (Perfection)

And many more.

In Vajrayana practice, a practitioner must cultivate until the illusory body appears before one dies.

Sometimes there can be more than one illusory body. When one has many illusory bodies, it is known as the "illusory bodies emanated beyond the flesh."

I personally believe that the best method to cultivate the illusory body is to practice the "Mirror Gazing Yoga."

I have discussed the "Mirror Gazing Yoga" in detail before, and will not repeat it again. The key points are:

The practitioner, the personal deity, and the reflection of the practitioner in the mirror merge into one.

The illusory body is born in the illusion within the illusion. This illusory body is the finest body within a practitioner's own body. The illusory body is the emanation of one's mind power, which is also known as the "mind-made body," or the "spiritual body."

I will share a secret. To achieve the fruition of Buddhahood, two elements must combine:

First, the illusory body.

Second, the pure light.

The fruition of Buddhahood is equal, deep, permanent, unique, wonderful, pure, bright, and with perfect enjoyment.

This is also the supreme Buddha-nature.

I would like everyone to pay attention to the Six Yogas of Naropa. One can refer to the Illusory Body Yoga and Clear Light Yoga in the six yogas. However, I believe that the best way to achieve the illusory body is through practicing the Mirror Gazing Yoga.

My illusory bodies are the emanations beyond the flesh. The trillions of emanation bodies manifested by the Buddha as cited in Buddhist sutras are equal to trillions of illusory bodies. I remember after my divine eye was opened by the Golden Mother of the Jade Pond, my illusory body appeared. My illusory body viewed my own past lives, and travelled to the twenty-eight heavens and through the Six Paths of Existence. This is the journey of my illusory body.

If one wants to see one's own illusory body, one must successfully cultivate the Mirror Gazing Yoga. Only then, can one see the illusory body in meditation.

As to whether in the future I will be able to become a buddha, bodhisattva, arhat, heruka, dharma protector, daka, dakini, or celestial deity, I will completely ignore and not think about the outcome.

Sheng-yen Lu

16. "Nothing Matters" Is the Key Point

Let me tell you a joke first!
A newly wed tenderly contemplated sending a romantic text message to her husband who was on a business trip, so she texted to her husband:
If you're sleeping, send me your beautiful dream.
If you're laughing, send me your smile.
If you're eating, send me a small piece.
If you're drinking wine, send me its bouquet.
If you're crying, send me your tears.
I love everything about you!
The husband replied very quickly:
I am sitting on the toilet right at this moment, what may I send to you?
I'll send you...
(Ha ha ha!)
I personally think that this gentleman does not understand humor. If it was me, I would have replied like this:
I'll send you gold.

I'll send you an egg roll.
I'll send you some ice cream.
I'll send you the pleasure of being relieved.
(Ha ha ha!)
Honestly, I would like to tell you, the greatest formula of cultivation is "Nothing Matters."

"Nothing Matters" is close to "Tao."

One must maintain a mind of "Nothing Matters," enjoying the feeling of "emptiness" and "brightness."

"Nothing Matters" is not being a fool.
"Nothing Matters" is not being an idiot.
"Nothing Matters" is not being a blockhead.
"Nothing Matters" is not being a vegetable.
"Nothing Matters" is not being unconscious.

"Nothing Matters" means one must maintain a clear mind at every moment, but also abide in the state of "void and tranquility" at the same time.

In short:

One reacts agilely, is happy and unhindered, and does not care about consequences.

For example:

I do my routine dharma practice each day, and practice "Analytical Meditation" steadfastly.

As to whether in the future I will be able to become a buddha, bodhisattva, arhat, heruka, dharma protector, daka, dakini, or celestial deity, I will completely ignore and not think about the outcome.

Others may insult you, ignore them.
Others may slander you, ignore them.
Others may frame you, ignore them.
Others may compliment you, ignore them.
Others may praise you, ignore them.
Others may award you, ignore them.

I just continue on with my own "Analytical Meditation."
Favorable circumstances, ignore them.
Adverse circumstances, ignore them.
There is neither inside nor outside; there is no north, south, east nor west; there is no true nor false; there is no reincarnation nor nirvana; there is no before nor after; there is no right nor wrong; there is no differentiation.
This is adapting to what comes naturally, then marvelous effects appear.
I pay no attention to the number of disciples whether it is none, one hundred, ten thousand, or hundreds of millions. Neither do I care whether the disciples come or go.
He he he!
Ha ha ha!
I completely ignore everything.
This is namely the "Brightness and Emptiness" in the key Great Perfection formulas. Because of the "Brightness and Emptiness," "Nothing Matters."

Without the teaching by a qualified master, I believe that practicing Vajrayana Buddhism will not be easy.

Sheng-yen Lu

17. The Fundamental Template of Vajrayana Cultivation

A typical Vajrayana sadhana contains the following steps:
First, respectfully pay homage.
Second, make offerings.
Third, chant the Fourfold Refuge Mantra.
Fourth, make repentance for one's sins.
Fifth, inspire to follow the Four Immeasurable Vows (Immeasurable Loving-kindness, Immeasurable Compassion, Immeasurable Joy, and Immeasurable Equanimity).
Sixth, beseech all buddhas to turn the dharma wheel.
Seventh, request the buddhas to remain in the saha world and not enter into nirvana.
Eighth, visualize emptiness.
Ninth, visualize the principal deity.
Tenth, recite the principal deity's mantra.
Eleventh, enter samadhi.
Twelfth, recite verses of praise.
Thirteenth, dedication.

Fourteenth, chant the Hundred Syllable Mantra (mending all faults).

Steps one to seven of the typical sadhana are known as the "preliminary practices;" steps eight to eleven are called "the main practices;" steps twelve to fourteen are known as "the concluding practices." This is a complete cultivation sadhana.

In general, lamas use this set of sadhanas for their daily cultivation.

In addition, it can be utilized for a blessing or bardo deliverance ceremony. (Recitation of sutras may be added.)

The sadhana can also be used for consecration and circumambulation of pagodas and temples. Many yogis secluded in mountain caves also practice with such rituals every day.

As for the higher level practices of cultivating qi, channels and light drops, or specializing in Inner Fire Yoga, the same sadhana can be used for petitioning:

Blessings from one's guru;

Blessings from one's principal deity;

Support from one's dharma protectors.

Of course, rituals are created by humans, so naturally one can recite additional sutras or mantras that one likes. If you are travelling by boat, aircraft or vehicle, of course, it is okay to only carry out "the main practices." All of these depend on the conditions and circumstances.

The four tantras requires one to learn the formal sadhana practices, such as setting up the altar (mandala), the skills to produce "offerings," the Action Tantra sadhana, the Performance Tantra sadhana, the Yoga sadhana, and the Highest Yoga Tantra sadhana.

In addition, the various principal deities all have their own different practices. Although the essentials of the practices are similar, there are some different features. One must pay attention to the differences, in order to differentiate each practice.

The practice of Guhyasamaja, Cakrasamvara, Hevajra, Yamantaka, Mahottara Heruka, Kalachakra, and others are not all identical.

There are similarities and differences. One must learn the subtle and profound characteristics of each practice.

No matter what sadhanas, the practitioner must have faith and a premise, which is inseparable from the "Three Principal Aspects of the Path" of Je Tsongkhapa:

First, supra-mundane-mind;

Second, bodhicitta;

Third, the Middle Way.

Although I have written so much today, each step of the sadhanas in fact has its own key formula. These numerous formulas are all accumulated from my past experience. Without the teaching by a qualified master, I believe that practicing Vajrayana Buddhism will not be easy.

I would like to tell a joke:

Not drinking any alcohol is the choice of a temperate person.

Drinking only a little is the mark of a gentleman.

Seeing alcohol and drinking impulsively is the path of an idiot.

Getting drunk every time one drinks is the way of a madman.

Driving drunk must be the son of Lord Yama.

Ha ha ha!

The knowledge regarding the word "alcohol" is quite profound!

To train one's ability to concentrate and subdue one's own arrogance are the most important.

Sheng-yen Lu

18. Benefits of Performing the Great Homage

A disciple asked me, "What are the benefits for the Tibetans who pay homage every three steps starting from their hometowns to the Jokhang and Ramoche Temples in Lhasa?"

I replied:

The homage that the Tibetans perform every three steps is a full prostration, which is different from the kowtow in the middle kingdom.

The former throws oneself flat on the ground face downward. (Full-body worship)

The latter kneels and touches the ground with the forehead. (Half-body worship)

The great homage of Tibetan Vajrayana Buddhism belongs to the former.

Most Tibetans perform the great homage while circumambulating and worshipping temples, pagodas, holy mountains, and holy lakes.

The benefits are:

To strengthen one's determination and perseverance for cultivation.

To accumulate provisions for cultivation.

To appreciate the value of being a human being.
To exercise one's physical body.
To sever evil deeds and carry out good deeds.
To train one's ability to concentrate.
To subdue one's own arrogance.
To form an affinity with buddhas.
And many more.

The disciple asked, "Wow, I have never thought of so many benefits! Grand Master Lu, which do you think are the most important?"

I thought for a moment and answered:

To train one's ability to concentrate and subdue one's own arrogance are the most important.

The reason is that when performing great homage, one concentrates on the head, hands, feet, and the whole body. Since every part of one's body works simultaneously, it is not easy for one to generate improper thoughts. Without improper thoughts one focuses wholeheartedly.

In addition, full prostration places a practitioner in a humble position. With the sky above one's head and the ground below one's face, the posture shows the most respect and one's arrogance will disappear.

The main purpose for practitioners in cultivating their minds is to eliminate their thoughts of greed, hate, stupidity, doubt, and arrogance.

If arrogant thoughts are not eliminated, pride will arise. We know that pride will lead one to the Path of Asuras, and the desire for competition and fighting. Fighting and competition can unconsciously turn one to evil.

The disciple asked, "Are there key points in paying great homage?"

I replied:

The following is my personal experience.

While paying great homage, I chant, "Homage to the 36 trillion, 119 thousand and 500 Amitabha Buddhas."

I visualize that trillions of emanation bodies of Amitabha Buddhas appear in the space before my eyes.

Performing a single prostration in such a manner is equal to chanting countless buddha epithets and simultaneously worshipping countless Amitabha Buddhas.

As a result, one will accumulate endless provisions and merits.

I would like to tell a joke:

A woman said to her husband, "We have been married for years. However, you have never say anything nice about me but only mention my shortcomings. You should mention some of my good attributes!"

Her husband replied, "Except for all the shortcomings, the rest is all good!"

The wife said, "Then say it! What good attributes do I have?"

The husband replied, "Oh, there's nothing to say!"

I mean to say:

A practitioner should perform more great homage, and talk less boring nonsense.

Tremendous motivation leads to tremendous merit.

Sheng-yen Lu

19. The Secret of Changing from One Offering to Many

In Vajrayana practice, there are several kinds of achievements. In summary, there are three major achievements:
First, mantra chanting accomplishment.
Second, homa accomplishment.
Third, samadhi accomplishment.
The first achievement is to chant mantras until the appearance of a great pure light.
The second achievement is to practice fire offerings until perfect completion of blessedness and virtue is achieved.
The third achievement is the great achievement of awakening the mind and seeing the Buddha-nature in samadhi.
Some people say, "In cultivation of Vajrayana Buddhism, it is all about making offerings, because the offering dharma is of primary importance."
There is a Great Mandala Offering in Vajrayana Buddhism. I think this offering practice condenses the universe into a mandala with magnificent offerings placed on the mandala.

The mandala has multiple layers:
The dharma wheel is erected at the top – a symbol of the highest light achievement of the universe.

Offerings are placed in the middle – these include gold, silver, jewelry, medicinal herbs, and rice.

At the bottom of the mandala – are stones and sand.

The Tibetan Vajrayana Buddhism sadhana for The Great Mandala Offering is complicated. (One should consult a vajra master for the details.)

There are also thirty-seven offerings,
Eight offerings in front of the holy shrine,
Five mounds of offerings,
Rice offering,
Water offering,
Fire offering,
And many more.

A disciple asked me, "What is the purpose of offering?"

I replied, "It is to accumulate provisions for blessings, virtue and wisdom."

The disciple asked, "What's the key point?"

I replied, "The key point is effort. One who provides strenuous efforts makes the best offering. Therefore, the merit of offering does not originate from the seven precious objects and eight treasures, but from the heart of oneself. Tremendous motivation leads to tremendous merit."

I have told my disciples that my experience is the following:

The Great Mandala Offering that I practice is "the body, speech, and mind are offered to the buddhas, bodhisattvas, vajra protectors, dakas and dakinis, all the devas, and beings in the Six Paths......."

Pure offering of body.
Mantra offering through speech.
Visualized offering within the mind.

As for offering food, one should offer all the foods before eating them. One should transform the foods into an expanse of offerings through one's mind power.

As for offering clothing, one should transform one's clothes into an expanse of offerings using one's mind power.

As for offering one's home, one should transform one's house, items, bedding, and everything into an expanse of offerings.

As for offering one's transportation, one should transform one's car and all means of transportation into an expanse of offerings.

Whenever one experiences pleasure, one should transform the happiness into an expanse of offerings.

One should transform jewelry, all the seven precious objects and eight treasures, into an expanse of offerings.

And so on and so forth… etc.

Honestly, I would like to tell all the disciples that one should transform everything, all one's behaviors, practices, and daily life activities, into an expanse of offerings, by transforming each and every one from one to many.

(This is the key formula)

I say:

In the future, if I reincarnate as a man, I will still be number one in the world:

I'll transform a piece of gold into a gold mountain.

I'll transform a little food into endless delicious foods.

I'll transform a piece of land into the whole planet earth.

I'll transform a beautiful woman into celestial maidens of the ten directions and three times.

I'll transform my single mind into numerous transformations. (Expansive bodhicitta aspirations)

I have become a buddha.

Persons of high scope take refuge to save sentient beings from the sea of suffering and effect universal deliverance.

Sheng-yen Lu

20. Opening the Door of Wisdom

The lives of modern people share a similar pattern. Don't you agree? Everyone's life is almost the same from birth to death.
Birth.
Infant stage.
Student stage.
Career stage.
Marriage stage.
Parenting stage.
Aging stage.
Death.
I often mention this:
One year old - making debuts.
Ten years old - preoccupied in school studies.
Twenty years old - Love is in the air.
Thirty years old - building careers.
Forty years old - getting stouter.
Fifty years old - geriatric prime.
Sixty years old - rising blood pressure.

Seventy years old - occasionally forgetful.
Eighty years old - swaying.
Ninety years old – losing direction.
A hundred years old - portrait on the wall.
There is not much difference for everyone; therefore, what does life mean to you?

I believe:

"Only by practicing Buddhism can we be liberated from all the afflictions in life. The Buddhadharma is the key to opening the door of wisdom. In order to end the cycle of reincarnation, to achieve nirvana, and to become an enlightened person, one must cultivate."

At the beginning of cultivation, one must first take refuge with a guru, the buddha, dharma, and sangha.

Persons of modest scope take refuge because they fear the pains associated with the animal realm, hungry ghost realm, and hell realm. They seek the comforts in the human world and the heavens.

Persons of medium scope take refuge aiming to stop the cycle of reincarnation and enter nirvana.

Persons of high scope take refuge to save sentient beings from the sea of suffering and effect universal deliverance.

In terms of growing faith in taking refuge:

Some people read my books and listened to my dharma discourses.

Some experienced spiritual responses, and their pains released by my blessings.

Some witnessed others who received spiritual responses.

I personally feel that many people have the initial resolve to seek enlightenment, but they don't have the spiritual perseverance, which is a common problem amongst human beings. If people do not have strong faith and a firm belief, most will give up halfway. People's minds often change, because the mind is impermanent. I often say people's minds are like water, flowing from one place to another. They take refuge with one master at one moment and with another at the next moment. They have faith in Buddhism at one moment, and then don't in the next moment. This is after all normal behavior, and not unexpected.

Therefore, there are rules in Vajrayana teachings:

One must recite over a hundred thousand times the Fourfold Refuge Mantra:

Namo Guru bei. (Take refuge in the guru)
Namo Buddha ye. (Take refuge in the buddha)
Namo Dharma ye. (Take refuge in the dharma)
Namo Sangha ye. (Take refuge in the sangha)

My taking refuge was triggered by the Golden Mother of the Jade Pond opening my divine eye. I saw the White Maha Padmakumara as my former life and his pure land, the Maha Twin Lotus Ponds. From that moment, I started to wholeheartedly study Buddhism, study the Buddhadharma, and behave virtuously.

The reasons that my faith has never wavered are:

First, I have truly "seen."

Second, I have spiritual responses.

Third, I have dharma power.

Fourth, I am able to save sentient beings.

Fifth, I have awakened the mind and seen the Buddha-nature.

Sixth, I have attained Buddhahood.

When in the future, my holy disciples reach the same attainments by firmly believing that Living Buddha Lian-sheng Sheng-yen Lu has indeed achieved the six abilities mentioned above and continuously practice the True Buddha Tantric Dharma, they will naturally never lose the faith. These are holy disciples truly with long lasting bodhicitta.

In order to save sentient beings, it is necessary for me to let disciples have spiritual responses, so that they will have strong faith.

The key point for disciples never giving up occurs when they have spiritual responses which induce faith.

Wise disciples should be able to see my tireless efforts and achievements.

If not, then continue to be like water flowing aimlessly, or get lost.

21. Reciting the Vajrasattva Mantra

I often teach people to recite the Vajrasattva Mantra:
The short form is: O*m, be-dza, sah-do, ah, hum, pei.*
The long form is the Hundred Syllable Mantra.

We know that the Primordial Buddha is the highest, the Five Dhyani Buddhas are below him, and finally there is Vajrasattva.

Therefore, Vajrasattva is the dharma prince of the Five Dhyani Buddhas.

Vajrayana Buddhism considers Vajrasattva as the founder.

The Vajrasattva Mantra has two major significances:

First, "emptiness."

Second, "brightness and emptiness."

Chanting the Hundred Syllable Mantra is the great dharma of repentance.

Why should one repent?

One should repent because sentient beings give rise to thoughts that manifest nothing but negative karma.

In addition, each person, in the present or countless past lives, has accumulated a great deal of negative karma. If one does not repent, the negative karma will become obstacles, which will prevent one from having achievments in their spiritual practice. Consequently, one will fall into the three evil paths.

This is the main reason for us to practice the dharma of repentance.

First, one should visualize that there is a white lotus flower with a thousand petals above one's crown chakra. On the white lotus is Vajrasattva in a father-mother form.

In the heart chakra of Vajrasattva, there is a Hum (ཧཱུྃ) syllable surrounded by the Hundred Syllable Mantra.

While reciting the Hundred Syllable Mantra, the practitioner visualizes the syllables transforming into a white nectar. The white nectar continuously flows into the practitioner's body through the crown chakra. As a result, all diseases within the body transform into black blood, all harmful obstructions transform into poisonous insects, and all negative karma transforms into black smoke.

The black blood, poisonous insects and black smoke are discharged from the skin pores, the anus and the soles of the feet.

The practitioner is purified and perfect.

One then recites the Hundred Syllable Mantra for seven times, 21 times, or 108 times. The more the better.

Finally, one recites the Repentance Verse.

I personally feel that the key formula for practicing repentance is: "To repent sincerely."

Repentance is not a formality, nor a ritual, but a practice one must perform wholeheartedly.

A sage once said, "All sins originate from the heart, so one should repent from the heart."

Vajrasattva made the following vow:

"If sentient beings commit the five cardinal sins, and have broken the Samaya Pledge, as long as they hear my epithet, have faith in me, and recite the king of mantras, which is the Hundred Syllable Mantra, then all hindrances will be cleared."

I believe that the Vajrasattva practice is the number one repentance dharma.

Finally, I would like to tell everyone these important key points:

If one's karmic hindrances have been eliminated by practicing repentance, auspicious signs must manifest. The auspicious signs can manifest as the following:

Dreams of eating a white substance and spitting out a black substance.

Dreams of expelling black blood and filth through the anus.

Dreams of poisonous insects crawling out from the skin pores.

Dreams of black smoke emitting from the body, or from the soles of the feet.

One sees that their body is transparent, radiating pure light.

One is standing on a lotus or riding upon a heavenly horse.

One is flying in the empty sky.

Dreams of Vajrasattva or one's personal deity placing their palm upon one's head.

Receiving a prediction from one's personal deity...

These are the auspicious signs from practicing the repentance dharma.

I would like to tell a joke:

A family was about to leave on a trip.

The wife was slowly choosing outfits to wear.

The husband was impatiently shouting, "Hurry up, stop putting off any more!" Their son interrupted, "Dad, Mother is putting on clothes, not putting off."

Ha ha ha!

Repentance should not be delayed!

Equanimity is the basis of developing bodhicitta, which is a heart with equality and without discrimination.

Sheng-yen Lu

22. The Pure Heart of Bodhicitta

Let me begin with a joke:
In order to test the loving compassion of a pupil, a teacher posed a question to the student, "What would you do if you are on a bus and see an old lady standing in front of you and is having difficulty moving?"

The student answered, "Old lady, you are already so old. No need to save any more money. Go take a taxi!"

(Ha ha ha!)

I often tell this story:

A professional robber attempted to steal from a village.

Upon entering the village, he noticed a baby who had just learned how to crawl was dangerously close to the edge of a well. The baby was only a step from falling into the well.

Instinctively, he stepped forward, picked up and placed the infant in a safe area.

Afterwards, the robber continued to the village to carry out the robbery.

My comment is that:

Even a robber has compassion.

As spiritual practitioners, we of course should develop the bodhicitta which includes the so-called Aspiration Bodhicitta, Action Bodhicitta, and Absolute Bodhicitta.

We often say:

To give people happiness – benevolence.

To remove people's sufferings - compassion.

To fulfill one's vows happily - joy.

To give equally without discrimination - equanimity.

I understand that the focus of a bodhisattva is on equanimity, which is the key point.

"Benevolence without specificity and great compassion based on sameness in essence" is not a hackneyed phrase, but means equanimity.

We are aware:

The human body leads to suffering.

The human world is a burning house.

Human beings are all so pitiful, especially those who are your enemies and those who hate you. They do not understand, have muddled thoughts, and are not awakened. Those who have resentment and hatred are even more pitiful.

You have to save them.

This is equanimity.

Equanimity is the basis of developing bodhicitta, which is a heart with equality and without discrimination.

Think of others without considering oneself.

This is called being a bodhisattva.

The key point of Aspiration Bodhicitta is - to "exchange oneself with others."

The key point of Action Bodhicitta is - the "wisdom of equality."

The key point of Absolute Bodhicitta is - "emptiness."

There are three ways to develop bodhicitta:

King-like bodhicitta – one achieves Buddhahood first, then helps others to achieve it.

Boatman-like bodhicitta – one reaches Buddhahood with other sentient beings.

Shepherd-like bodhicitta – one helps others to achieve Buddhahood before one achieves it.

In this life I, Living Buddha Lian-sheng Sheng-yen Lu, descended to the saha world to save sentient beings. The main purpose is to play a role in a drama of saving sentient beings that includes:

Donating wealth - to the Sheng-Yen Lu Foundation.

Teaching Buddhadharma – through numerous dharma disseminations and empowerments.

Bestowing fearlessness – to help others cross to the other shore together.

Five precepts - to prevent misconduct.

Ten good deeds – to benefit sentient beings.

Bearing insults – others and oneself are equal.

Perseverance – laziness and lethargy must be abandoned.

Meditation – being detached to everything.

Wisdom – listening, contemplating and cultivating Buddhadharma to cross to the other shore.

This is a drama of saving sentient beings. When the drama is over, it will be time for me to leave!

Ha ha ha!

The Buddhadharma benefits both human and celestial realms, therefore producing the greatest merits and field of blessings.

Sheng-yen Lu

23. What Merits the Greatest Field of Blessings?

I recall a joke that goes like this:
A student said to a math teacher, "My father would like to listen to your lecture. Is it okay?"

The math teacher replied, "Certainly, is he interested in math?"

The student answered, "No! My father thinks that sleeping is the greatest blessing!"

The math teacher asked, "What does sleeping have to do with mathematics?"

The student answered, "My father is a chronic insomniac. All treatments have been useless. After hearing how I can easily fall asleep in your math class, he wants to come and try!"

Ha ha ha!

The greatest field of blessings for the father is sleep!

What bears the greatest field of blessings for practitioners?

I believe it is:

To pray for buddhas to remain in the saha world.

To pray for buddhas to turn the dharma wheel.

This yields the greatest field of blessings.

Some people think that giving produces the greatest field of blessings. This is also correct, as one can receive the karmic merits of the Heavens through giving.

Some people think that providing offerings to the Sangha will produce the greatest field of blessings. This is also correct, as providing offerings to the Sangha, one will gather a great field of blessings, and easily receive the blessings of buddhas and bodhisattvas.

Some people think that taking care of sick people will produce the greatest field of blessings. This is also correct, as sickness is the most painful thing. If one can remove the sufferings of patients, the virtues and merits are naturally great.

However, for one to truly earn the greatest field of blessings is:

To pray for buddhas to remain in the saha world.

To pray for buddhas to turn the dharma wheel.

This occurs because only by so doing, the Buddhadharma will exist in the saha world.

The Buddhadharma benefits both human and celestial realms, therefore producing the greatest merits and field of blessings.

If there is no Buddhadharma, what is the field of blessings?

I remember that:

When Shakyamuni Buddha was about to enter nirvana, there was a layman named Cunda who prayed for the Buddha to remain in the saha world.

The Buddha delayed his entering into nirvana for three months and discoursed one more significant sutra.

Moreover:

Immediately after achieving enlightenment under the bodhi tree for forty-nine days, Shakyamuni Buddha only wanted to liberate himself into nirvana without teaching the Buddhadharma or saving sentient beings.

Then, Maha Brahma and Indra descended.

They offered the Buddha a right spiral conch and a golden wheel.

They beseeched the Buddha to expound the dharma.

The Buddha then spoke the dharma and turned the dharma wheel. In this way, Buddhism was able to spread throughout the world. This really merits the greatest field of blessings!

Which one is greater, a worldly field of blessings or a supramundane field of blessings?

My key formula on the field of blessings is:
To pray for buddhas to remain in the saha world.
To pray for buddhas to turn the dharma wheel.
This is the greatest formula for the perfect accomplishment of provisions.

I composed two verses:
Field of blessings, field of blessings
Chased by everyone diligently
Accumulation of gold, silver and treasures
None can be carried away from the world
Additionally...
Field of blessings, field of blessings
Is not as good as having karmic affinity with a buddha
Pray for buddhas to turn the dharma wheel
Merits will manifest before one's eyes
This is the true formula for the greatest field of blessings!

In a condition free of any state whatsoever, there is no need to explain anything.

Sheng-yen Lu

24. The Nature of Absolute Emptiness

I would like to tell a joke first that is related to the topic:
Mr. Wang opened a coffin store.
A customer entered and asked, "This coffin is half the price of the other coffin, but I looked carefully and found no difference between the two!"
Mr. Wang replied, "The two coffins look almost the same, but the expensive one was designed according to the shape of a human body that allows people to rest more comfortably. Do you want to try?"
The customer was stunned and speechless.
Ha ha ha!
What I mean to say is, once people pass away and return to the state of emptiness, what is comfortable? What is uncomfortable?
I say:
After one passes away, everything stops and the body rests in quiescence.
In Vajrayana Buddhism, one often learns to "observe emptiness," "meditate" and "enter into the state of samadhi."
This is the nature of the absolute emptiness.
The key formula of body – is being immovable.

The key formula of speech – is being silent.
The key formula of mind - is being tranquil.
Accomplishing these three points, one reaches the nature of the absolute emptiness.
These three points look easy, but are quite difficult to achieve.
In regards to the body:
One avoids all earthly things, does not even attempt Buddhist activities, and meditates motionlessly in the full lotus position.
In regards to speech:
One remains silent which includes not reciting mantras audibly or silently.
In regards to the mind:
One ceases all delusive thoughts, does not think about the past, present, nor the future, and is not confused. Everything ceases suddenly.
One does not visualize the personal deity nor the shrine.
One does not observe the mind, nor is attached to any thoughts.
(It seems that this is the most difficult part, since people generally have a lot of wandering thoughts. Even thoughts are not allowed.)
Contemplation of ending thoughts is not even allowed.
This is the nature of the absolute emptiness.
This is:
"No beginning or end."
"No birth or death."
"Naturally so, naturally so."
"The absolute emptiness and the absolute emptiness."
(This is light and the illusory body uniting together.)
This is also:
The light and Buddha-nature.
Not forgetting and not attaching.
Existing at all times and without discrimination.
Marvelous existence and excellent emptiness.

In a condition free of any state whatsoever, there is no need to explain anything. Since it is ineffable and indefinable, any explanation will be meaningless.

In this condition, all sentient beings can be subdued. This turns into quiescence, eliminates confusion, increases virtues, enables fearlessness, creates blessings, enlightens, liberates sentient beings, nurtures compassion, and awakens supernatural powers ......

This key formula is "naturally so."

This is "non-grasping and non-attachment."

This is also what Manjushri Bodhisattva referred to as:

"The body, mind, dharma, and nature are all empty."

If one practices these three dharmas properly and precisely, it is very easy for one to enter the analytical meditation of the completion stage.

Sheng-yen Lu

25. The Leading Practices of the Vajrayana Completion Stage

I have explained much about the Vajrayana completion stage during my dharma discourses. Most of the essential key points have been described in detail. For example:
Channels, qi, light drops,
The Nine Cycle Breathing Exercise,
Vajra Chanting,
Treasure Vase Breathing Practice,
Inner Fire,
Light drops.
I have elaborated on the above practices, and the key points can be found throughout my dharma talks. One must not take those key points as only knowledge, but practice them earnestly and steadfastly.
For example:
The Nine Cycle Breathing Exercise consists of three variations of visualization and breathing. Each variation requires three repetitions.
The key points are:
Concentration.

Power of Mindfulness.
Breathing gently, slowly, and long.
Why should one breathe gently - the key point is to be "meticulous."
Why should one breathe slowly - the key point is to be "tranquil."
Why should one breathe long - the key point is to "enter quietude."
Moreover:
Vajra Chanting visualizes the syllables (ༀ) "om," (ཨཱཿ) "ah," and (ཧཱུྃ) "hum."
Om - Represents the blessing of the buddhas of the three times (in white).
Ah - Represents the words of the buddhas of the three times (in red).
Hum - Represents the mind of the buddhas of the three times (in blue).
We know that Vajra Chanting is the Vajrayana unification cultivation of chanting, visualization, and holding the qi.
First, breathe in; second, hold your breath; third, breathe out.
I would like to inform you:
These three seed syllables have great merit, which can change one's fate.
The key points of the three seed syllables are:
Om (Dharma Body).
Ah (Bliss Body).
Hum (Emanation Body).
One breathes in the short seed syllable "om," holds the breath with the "ah" seed syllable for a period of time, then breathes out slowly the "hum" seed syllable.
The main purpose of the practice is to enter the stage of quietude, and then to progress to the stage of no birth.
In addition:
The Treasure Vase Breathing Practice is an internal qi practice, in which one visualizes three channels.

First, gently force downward the Ascending Qi, then raise upward the Descending Qi. The two streams of qi merge under the navel, forming a vase-like shape.

There are four stages in this practice:

Guiding – one breathes in air long and deeply down to the lower abdomen, and raises the Descending Qi, then the air and qi merge.

Filling – one holds the breath for thirty seconds, the longer the better.

Expelling - one visualizes the qi expelling out of one's skin pores.

Projecting – one visualizes the qi projecting to the top of the head, and then releasing through the nose.

Key points:

Force the qi to flow into the middle channel. This is called transmuting the expedient qi to the wisdom qi.

Safety precautions:

One should use the nostrils to breathe in and out. Do not practice when one is sick. One should not perform the four stages more than 21 cycles. The best time to perform the practice is in the early morning on an empty stomach.

Important note:

As there are differences in the practice for males and females, one must consult a vajra master for more information. Furthermore, the practice involves risks. One must not take it lightly and be cautious when practicing.

I personally think that the "Nine Cycle Breathing Exercise," "Vajra Chanting," and the "Treasure Vase Breathing Practice" are very important.

If one practices these three dharmas properly and precisely, it is very easy for one to enter the analytical meditation of the completion stage. The three practices are the key, and also the leading practices of the completion stage. I have explained this very clearly in my dharma talks.

The three dharmas all have complex key formulas. If one wishes to learn them in depth, one should purchase my DVD dharma talks.

I would like to tell a joke:

A lady said to her husband, "A lot of men say I have a pretty face and fit body. You never say that to me."

Her husband replied, "Well, you know, I don't like to tell jokes."

Ha ha ha!

(I too am not telling a joke! I am serious. These three practices are very important.)

26. Attaining Buddhahood through Qi Entering the Central Channel

In this article, I will briefly explain how the qi enters the central channel, enabling one to reach the state of Buddhahood. Please read all sentences carefully because each sentence is a key formula.

First, one guides qi into the central channel, which transforms the expedient qi into wisdom qi. One visualizes one's principal deity at the brow-point.

(Hold the qi for a period of time, visualize one's principal deity rising and manifesting.)

Second, the practitioner becomes the principal deity.

(At this point, the practitioner shows divine pride and focuses on the principal deity.)

Third, the principal deity descends to the navel chakra. At this moment, one chants a mantra silently and performs the Treasure Vase Breathing Practice.

One guides the "Ascending Qi" and "Descending Qi" to gather at the navel chakra. One uses the techniques of squeezing, pressing, and rubbing to ignite one's inner fire.

Squeezing. (To accumulate qi)
Pressing. (To hold tightly)
Rubbing. (Friction)
These are important key points, which can cause one's inner fire to ignite.

Fourth, the inner fire rises to the ajna chakra and dissolves the white light drops. The white light drops descend along the central channel, which evokes the feeling of the Four Blisses.

The preliminary bliss. (As the white light drops enter the throat chakra)

The excellent bliss. (As the white light drops enter the heart chakra)

The superior bliss. (As the white light drops enter the navel chakra)

The absolute bliss (As the white light drops enter the sacral chakra)

Fifth, one reverses the flow of the light drops along the central channel back to the ajna chakra, resulting in the Four Levels of Emptiness. These Four Levels of Emptiness also include the feeling of the Four Blisses.

(The simultaneous sensations present the bliss and emptiness as nondual and yet not distinct.)

Sixth, one visualizes the principal deity at one's navel chakra with a physical or an imagined consort, the white light drops within the firm vajra scepter and the red light drops at the crown chakra result in a feeling of bliss.

(This evokes the feeling of bliss)

Seventh, one accumulates all the white and red light drops in the central channel, layer by layer like a multi-layered cake.

As long as a small amount of light drops are gathered together, a small amount of bliss will be generated, which will eliminate some karmic hindrances.

The practitioner achieves Buddhahood through the manifestation of the principal deity.

(At this point, the red and white light drops have accumulated completely inside the central channel.)

Pay attention to these steps:

The principal deity and the consort of the principal deity become unified. The inner fire dissolves the white light drops at the ajna chakra, causing the white light drops to descend to the tip of the vajra scepter. This evokes the magnificent feeling of the Four Blisses.

Then, one reverses the flow of the light drops along the central channel back to the ajna chakra. This evokes the extraordinary feeling of the Four Blisses and Four Levels of Emptiness.

The white light drops mentioned here are referring to the body's secretion of hormones, the red light drops are referring to the inner fire.

The emptiness is the illusory body.

The form is the light.

My personal experience related to this practice is as follows:

Qi entering into the central channel is essential.

Igniting the inner fire is essential.

Dissolving the light drops is essential.

Descending of the light drops is essential.

Ascending of the light drops is essential.

Opening of the five chakras is essential.

Manifestation of the principal deity is essential.

Unification of emptiness and form is essential.

(Unification of the illusory body and pure light is the state of Buddhahood.)

Someone may ask me:

"In this article, why don't you mention that the father-mother practice is essential? Since the father-mother practice can cause the inner fire to ascend, and the light drops to descend, why don't you mention it?"

My response is:

"Human beings are the most troublesome creatures. If the father-

mother practice is mentioned, these creatures will create a clamour." Humans are the most troublesome beings.
Ha ha ha!

27. Protection Practices (Part I)

Generally, a protection practice occurs at the end of the Preliminary Practices. But, when necessary in daily life, the practice can be performed independently. Guarding oneself and one's residence is very important.

I have taught everyone:
Form the Vajra Mudra.
Recite the mantra, "*Om, bo-ru-lan-ze, lee.*"
Bring the Vajra Mudra to touch five different locations: head, throat, heart, left shoulder, and right shoulder.
Then, visualize Vajrapani Bodhisattva illuminating oneself; or oneself transforming into Vajrapani Bodhisattva.
This is the Armour Protection Method.
In addition, there are other methods to guard oneself:
In the first method, one chants the personal deity's heart mantra, and visualizes the deity on top of one's head transforming into a moon disc.
One visualizes the following three consecutive times: the moon disc dissolves into nectar, which descends into the practitioner's body drop by drop. The practitioner's body becomes the white color of the

moon disc.

One then recites, "All phenomena of self and others are originally pure."

In the second method, one visualizes Vairocana Buddha between the eyebrows, Amitabha Buddha in the throat chakra, Akshobhya Buddha in the heart chakra, Ratnasambhava Buddha in the navel chakra, and Amoghasiddhi Buddha in the sacral chakra.

One can also visualize the seed syllables of the five buddhas.

One then visualizes oneself transforming into Vajrasattva.

Then one recites this mantra, "*Om, be-dza, sah-do, ah, hum-pei.*"

In the third method, one recites the karma eradication mantra of the Seven Buddhas. One then cleanses the hands, before visualizing; one's the right hand transforming into the moon, and the left hand transforming into the sun.

Place the palms together, and visualize a blue-green "hum" (ཧཱུྃ) syllable appearing within the palms of the sun and moon. The syllable then transforms into a vajra scepter.

Touch the head, throat, heart, navel, sacral chakra, both shoulders, and feet with the vajra scepter (the palms).

Recites one's personal deity's mantra.

Visualize oneself and one's personal deity unified, abiding in the personal deity's divine pride.

In the fourth method, one visualizes oneself transforming into the personal deity. The personal deity's seed syllables then cover one's body, and one becomes the personal deity's original nature of indestructible vajra.

One then is protected by the personal deity wearing vajra armor or with powerful weapons.

In the fifth method, the practitioner's own channels, chakras, joints, etc., are all covered with sacred syllables.

The syllables transform into vajra scepters.

Each vajra scepter emits the five colors, not only shining on oneself, but also shining on all evil obstructions in the ten directions.

The evil obstructions in the ten directions are thereby destroyed.

Above are the methods of cultivating protection. The key point is transforming the mudras, visualizations, and syllables into wisdom.

I would like to share a joke:

A man said, "Every time I have a problem with my wife, we end up feeling thirsty."

His friend said, "You two must be swearing and yelling at each other too much!"

The man replied, "No, we don't even say one word."

His friend then asked, "How can that happen?"

The man replied, "This is because we just spit on each other!"

(Ha ha ha!)

When facing evil obstructions, we do not need to swear nor spit. We just cultivate the practices that protect ourselves. One will then be thoroughly purified.

The key points are:

Purity.

Indestructibility.

Firmness.

At the end, the practitioner needs to provide offerings to all the spiritual guardians.

Sheng-yen Lu

28. Protection Practices (Part II)

In this chapter, I will continue to discuss the protection practices regarding a residence.
In the past, I have taught:
The vajra foundation.
The vajra wall.
The vajra flaming wall.
The vajra net.
Above is one of the residence protection methods.
Another method that I often practice is reciting the Nine-character Mantra while placing the palms together. I happen to practice this method every half month.
I bless everywhere in the house reciting "*Lin, bing, dou, zhe, jie, zhen, lie, zai, qian,*" which not only cleans and eradicates all evil hindrances, but also completely expels all the demons and evil spirits inside the residence.
The following is a Tibetan Buddhism practice:
Establish an emptiness shrine first; then followed by a wind shrine in a half-moon shape in the middle; and a triangle fire altar above. (Three characters of emptiness, wind, and fire.)

Subsequently, a protection wheel rises with a foundation below. Five-layered walls then appear.

Each protective wall is fully covered with swords and spears to prevent invasions from ghosts and evil spirits.

A vajra net suspended in the air protects from above.

A vajra foundation is underneath.

Vajra walls surround the four sides with sharp weapons or fire covering the walls.

Within the space visualized above is a vajra palace and in the center of the palace is a "dharma throne."

The practitioner is cultivating on a sun-disc pad that is on the lotus dharma throne.

(The above visualization is used to protect a residence)

One then invokes dharma protectors to descend one by one from the void.

The dharma protectors may be:

The ten wrathful Wisdom Kings.

The ten Removal Protectors.

The ten Constellations Deities.

The ten Dragon Kings.

The ten ghost subjugating deities.

These spiritual guardians are invoked to protect the practitioners during their cultivation. Each one of these protectors stands guard around the residence.

(The positioning of these protectors is similar to the illustrations in a Mandala.)

The practitioner transforms into the personal deity.

Throughout these complicated procedures, proper manifestations rely on clear visualization.

At the end, the practitioner needs to provide offerings to all the spiritual guardians.

These offerings can include purified and blessed meat, liquor, water and many other offerings.

Please pay attention. During our dharma ceremonies, we have often photographed prajna lights. If one enlarges the image of these prajna lights and looks closely, one will notice that each prajna light contains a deity in the center and the deity is surrounded by dharma protectors.

In other words, every prajna light is a manifestation of a deity's abode.

Moreover, when travelling by air, some practitioners have taken beautiful photographs of their plane surrounded by rainbow lights.

The phenomenon is a manifestation of the honorable guardians protecting the practitioners in the aircraft.

The key points are:

Clear visualization.

Correct sadhana.

Sincere offerings.

All the behaviors and dignity of a practitioner are the pure manifestation from the wisdom of great bliss of the principal deity.

Sheng-yen Lu

29. Falling Asleep and Waking Up

I used to teach Dream Yoga this way:
Before sleeping, one visualizes a syllable "ཧྲཱིཿ" (seh) at the throat chakra.
The syllable transforms into Amitabha Buddha.
Amitabha Buddha emits red light that projects into the void like fireworks expanding into a magnificent parasol.
The red light parasol gradually descends and covers the body of the practitioner.
One then falls asleep. This practice is one form of Dream Yoga.
Alternatively:
Before sleeping, one visualizes that Vairocana Buddha is located at one's ajna chakra, Amitabha Buddha at the throat chakra, Akshobhya Buddha at the heart chakra, Ratnasambhava Buddha at the navel chakra, and Amoghasiddhi Buddha at the sacral chakra.
One may also visualize the corresponding seed syllables of the five buddhas respectively at the chakras instead.
All the buddhas emit light.
The practitioner thus sleeps in the five colors of light. This is also a Dream Yoga.

Moreover:

Before sleeping, one visualizes a syllable "rang" that sets one's whole body on fire, burning the body into ashes.

One then visualizes a syllable "yang" and the ashes are blown away by the wind. The practitioner's body becomes like the empty void.

Finally, the practitioner visualizes a syllable "kang" and everything disappears.

This is equal to a drop of water merging into the sea, or unification of the child light with the mother light, which implies that a small light is assimilated into a big light.

This is another form of Dream Yoga.

Meanwhile:

Upon waking, one visualizes that dakinis are playing damarus that produce dong, dong, dong sounds.

One may also visualize goddesses playing celestial music.

The dakinis or goddesses persuade the practitioner to emerge from the light meditation.

The practitioner transforms into the principal deity.

Above are all the key formulas.

In the teachings of Mahayoga:

All the behaviors and dignity of a practitioner are the pure manifestation from the wisdom of great bliss of the principal deity.

Everyone around the practitioner becomes a heavenly being of the principal deity.

The entire outside world transforms into celestial palaces and castles.

All visualizations in one's mind become a mandala.

Again, these are all key formulas.

After succeeding in the development stage, we should enter the completion stage.

Since the completion stage is supramundane, it enables a practitioner to transform into an enlightened buddha.

I will make an analogy by relating a joke:

If I were a leader who plans to win the World Cup of Football, I would select a group of twenty-year-old strong young men who have been sentenced to death.

I would have them trained to play football for several years.

Then I would let them play for the World Cup.

If they win, they would be set free.

If they lose, they would be executed.

Now that it is a game of life and death, I can say that this would guarantee that they will win!

I observe that we Buddhist practitioners are the same. We must strive to cultivate.

If we are unsuccessful – we remain in the cycle of life and death.

If we are successful – we become a buddha.

If you are willing to suffer in the six realms of transmigration, again and again going through the life imprisonment, you do not need to cultivate.

Through such cultivation, it is very easy for a practitioner to accomplish the Path of Accumulation, attain selflessness, and achieve emptiness.

Sheng-yen Lu

30. Body Offering

I would like to first share some facts.

In Tibet, no matter how hard one tries, it is impossible to boil a pot of water. This shows that one's "environment" is very important.

When riding a bicycle, no matter how hard one tries, it is impossible to catch a motorcycle. This shows that "equal status" is very important.

A man, no matter how impressive who he is, without a woman, cannot have a baby. This reveals that "cooperation" is very important.

No matter how capable a person is, it is difficult to compete against a group of people. This shows that "teamwork" is very important.

If one wants water to drink, no matter how large a bucket, it is not as good as digging a well. This shows that "resources" are very important.

If one wants to receive the five blessings, one must believe in cause and effect, pay attention to moral cultivation, be virtuous and bear the utmost onerous duties. This shows that one's "behavior" is very important.

In order to attain achievement, one must sincerely change their actions, thoughts, and mind. This shows that one's "mentality" is very important.

Two frogs fell in love. After getting married, they gave birth to a toad. The father frog was furious. The mother frog cried and said that she had plastic surgery before the marriage. This shows that "understanding" is very important.

A young donkey said to an old donkey that we eat grass every day but the dairy cow eats special feed every meal! The old donkey sighed and said that we rely on our legs to make a living, and the cow relies on its udders to make a living. This shows that "conditions" are very important.

A duck raced a crab, and at the end it was difficult to tell who the winner was. A referee decided that they should play rock-paper-scissors to determine who would be the winner. The duck was furious, because the duck could only show paper, and the crab would always show scissors. This shows that "innateness" is very important.

A dog asked a bear to marry him and promised the bear that she would be happy. The bear replied that if I married you, our offspring would be a black bear. I wanted to marry a cat so that I would have a distinguished panda bear. This shows that "selection" is very important.

My purpose of sharing the above is mainly to explain the following:

Giving results in the largest provisions. Good fortune comes from charity. In order to receive the greatest blessings, one needs to give completely. What is to give completely? Offering one's body! This is the greatest blessing. This shows that the practice of body offering is of greatest importance.

The practice of body offering is as follows:

First, one visualizes one's own light drop, as big as a bean, flying up to the void. While one recites the syllable "Pei," the light drop transforms into a Krodha Kali, a black wrathful emanation of Machig Labdron.

The Krodha Kali holds a kartika in the right hand, a kapala (skull cap) in the left hand, and a khatvanga in the crook of the left arm.

The practitioner lies supine, and visualizes that the body is a corpse as big as the universe.

The practitioner then visualizes that the Krodha Kali severs the head of the corpse with the kartika and erects the head on three poles.

There is raging fire under the head.

The practitioner's head transforms into a skull cap.

Krodha Kali continues to dismember the corpse with the kartika. While she is burning each piece one by one, all pieces of the corpse become a nectar.

The syllable "Hang" becomes a white nectar.

The syllable "Ah" becomes a red nectar.

The practitioner offers the red and white nectar to one's guru, principal deity, and dharma protectors first.

The practitioner then offers the red and white nectar to the beings in the Six Paths and one's karmic enemies.

This makes the guru, principal deity, and dharma protectors happy.

This makes the practitioner's karmic enemies leave happily.

This makes the ghosts and gods happy.

(While visualizing, one chants "om-ah-hum," the three syllable mantra.)

This practice teaches one to sacrifice oneself.

This practice helps one to develop the bodhicitta.

The practitioner completely abandons themselves, and becomes an offering.

The practitioner eliminates their greed, anger, ignorance and so on.

Through such cultivation, it is very easy for a practitioner to accomplish the Path of Accumulation, attain selflessness, and achieve emptiness.

All the formulas in this practice are vast and perfect.

The biggest giving is the greatest blessing!

In the state of being half awake and half dreaming, I felt that my mind was very clear.

Sheng-yen Lu

31. A Stick of Burning Incense

In a small room, I first lit a stick of incense before turning off the lights and closing the curtains. The whole room now was completely dark, except for a red spot from the burning incense.

I sat in a natural position focusing my eyes on the little red spot of the burning incense.
Without deliberately focusing.
Neither a scattered mind.
I was just looking at the little red spot naturally.
If my mind inadvertently shifted away, I would pull it back to the little red spot.
I was sitting with a mind fully relaxed.
I did not contemplate.
I did not think.
Regardless of the length of time, whether long or short.
So I sat. (Without intention)
Later, unexpectedly that red spot enlarged, becoming bigger and bigger. The whole room was full of red spots.
First each red spot increased one by one, and then more and more appeared until the whole room became red.

Finally, even my body fully integrated with the little red spots. I became unified with the red light.

I was sitting naturally.

I had become the red light.

Unexpectedly my body, speech and mind resided in the nature state. All delusions stopped completely, and I entered the state of meditation.

The key points are as follows:

Body - one should not move.

Speech - one should not speak.

Mind - one should not think.

My God! In the state of being half awake and half dreaming, I felt that my mind was very clear.

I actually saw the world outside the room. There was a visitor in the living room downstairs, who came to see me.

I naturally opened the door of the small room, waiting for him.

He asked, "How do you know that I am coming?"

I replied, "I saw you!"

He asked, "How could you see me?"

I replied, "One stick of incense."

He was confused!

Ha ha ha!

From the "nature state" that I entered after lighting one stick of incense, I could actually see the world outside, people, things, the future, empty space, Buddha-lands, visitors coming from the empty space, and much more.

I would like to tell you a joke:

A man with a heavy heart was drinking at a bar.

A waiter asked him, "Sir, you look upset. Are you worried? Please share with us."

The man said, "I'm gay."

"So what?"

"My older brother is also gay."
The waiter was speechless.
The man continued, "Even worse, my younger brother is gay too."
"In your whole family, no one likes women?"
"Yes, my sister."
Ha ha ha!
Let me tell everyone! From one stick of incense, one red spot, I can actually see the mind of a human being. Through a glance, I know what a man is thinking.
Furthermore, I can see this person's future...

One becomes extremely peaceful and happy when one's body and mind are filled with emptiness, bliss, brilliance and wisdom.

Sheng-yen Lu

32. Subtle Key Cultivation Formulas for Light Drops

I remember that my guru gave me a crystal ball when I visited him in the past. His intention was for me to begin the practice of light drops.

The procedure for cultivating light drops is as follows:
Visualize the syllable "Om" at one's ajna chakra.
Visualize the syllable "Ah" at one's throat chakra.
Visualize the syllable "Hum" at one's heart chakra.
Visualize the syllable "Ho" at one's navel chakra.
Visualize the syllable "Hang" at one's sacral chakra.
Visualize the syllable "Ha" at one's crown chakra.
Visualize the syllable "Pei" at the tip of one's root.

The key points are as follows:
One visualizes the power from the two roots, which ignites the inner fire. One then guides the Descending Qi to enable the inner fire to rise through the central channel to the ajna chakra. As a result, the Bodhicitta Moon Fluid descends. When the light drops descend to the throat chakra, the preliminary bliss occurs. Superior bliss, most

superior bliss and innate bliss happen when the light drops descend to the heart chakra, navel chakra and the tip of the Vajra Pestle respectively. (This is the process for the descending of light drops.)

Conversely:

One experiences four levels of emptiness when the light drops are raised from the tip of the root up to the ajna chakra. One can also feel the four levels of bliss when experiencing the four levels of emptiness. (This is the process for raising the light drops.)

When the flow of the light drops is reversed back to the navel chakra, one achieves the homogenous production.

When the flow of the light drops is reversed back to the heart chakra, one achieves the result of maturation.

When the flow of the light drops is reversed back to the throat chakra, one achieves the results of experience.

When the flow of the light drops is reversed back to the brow chakra, one achieves the cessation effect.

I would like to state the following:

Both the descending and raising process can cause continuous and unlimited bliss. One can experience "the mind and cognition of emptiness" through the feeling of great bliss. This is the most superior attainment. Bliss and emptiness are the foundation of the Buddha's illusory bodies.

The important key points are as follows:

Inner fire - the power of the two roots.

Qi - the power of circulation.

Channels - the power of the paths of transportation.

Light drops - the power of cultivation and visualization.

Bliss - the power of sensation.

Emptiness - the power of realization.

The state of Buddhahood is a combination of brilliant light and emptiness.

The most refined body consists of the combination of great bliss, brilliant light, and emptiness.

Some disciples asked me, "There are nine divisions and four divisions in Vajrayana teachings, which one is correct?"

I replied, "Both are correct."

Some disciples have asked, "What do the Father Tantra and the Mother Tantra mean in Vajrayana Buddhism?"

I replied, "The Father Tantra represents expedient teachings, while the Mother Tantra represents wisdom."

Some disciples have asked, "What is the difference between Sutrayana and Vajrayana Buddhism?"

I answered, "Sutrayana Buddhism is the Bodhisattva Vehicle, which belongs to the Causal Vehicle. Vajrayana Buddhism is the Diamond Vehicle, which is the Resultant Vehicle. These two are inseparable. In Sutrayana Buddhism, one cultivates the cause to attain Buddhahood. In Vajrayana Buddhism, one cultivates the effect to attain Buddhahood. Sutrayana Buddhism is also the most important foundation for cultivating Vajrayana Buddhism."

I would like to tell my disciples:

A method that I learned in the past is one must take a breath to expand the fire while visualizing a fierce inner fire burning the Bodhicitta Moon Fluid at the brow-point. More light drops thereby will melt.

Taking a breath is essential each time practicing the step.

One's body thereafter is full of white light drops.

One becomes extremely peaceful and happy when one's body and mind are filled with emptiness, bliss, brilliance and wisdom.

From the extreme peace and happiness, one enters into a state of deep meditation. At the same time, one's whole body is full of white light and qi.

One resides in the expansive brilliant light.

(This is of utmost importance! Utmost importance!)

Then, from this light, many small white five-pronged vajra scepters flew out, filled the worlds of the ten directions, and destroyed the four maras of heaven, death, the Five Skandhas, and afflictions.

Sheng-yen Lu

33. To Achieve Peace of Mind

I would like to impart a key formula to achieve peace of mind based on a personal experience. Through the experience, I entered meditation and underwent the greatest and most incomparable peace and happiness.

I visualized the following:

Atop my crown chakra were my personal deity Amitabha Buddha and his Buddha Mother perched on a lotus.

The stem of the lotus inserted into the crown chakra that connects to my central channel.

The Amitabha Buddha and Buddha Mother were in unification.

Through the lotus stem and the crown chakra, white nectar filled the central channel.

The white nectar filled the five chakras.

The white nectar filled the channels and chakras of my whole body.

At last, the white nectar filled all the pores of my body.

My body was now full of white light drops.

During this process, I had been continuously reciting:

"*Om, a-mee-deh-wah, seh.*"

I sat in the posture of Amitabha Buddha.

The key formula is:
Body – Amitabha's mudra.
Speech – Amitabha's heart mantra.
Mind – Amitabha's visualization.
(Amitabha Buddha and the Buddha Mother in a father-mother form released white nectar that completely filled one's body.)
Thereby, my body, speech and mind became purified.
I then entered into a meditation of peace and happiness.
At this time, my body transformed into a five-pronged vajra scepter. The top of the five-pronged vajra scepter reached up to the Brahma Heaven, and the bottom down to the earth's vajra foundation.
The five-pronged vajra scepter radiated white light, which spun around the vajra scepter.
All evil and enemies were now incapable of harming.
Then, from this light, many small white five-pronged vajra scepters flew out, filled the worlds of the ten directions, and destroyed the four maras of heaven, death, the Five Skandhas, and afflictions.
Finally, the little white vajras scepters returned back into the large one.
I entered into a state of incomparable peace and happiness!
Disciples have asked:
"Isn't this kind of peace and happiness achieved by Grand Master Lu just a figment of your imagination?"
I answered:
"Vajrayana is cultivated expediently by the ritual procedures using both physical and dharma bodies. Through constant practice, the purely visualized physical and dharma bodies can become a reality."
I continued:
"All the supreme light, nectar, five-pronged vajra scepter, great bliss sensation, white light, and small vajra scepters are able to be induced through spiritually unified cultivation, especially the blessing and bestowing power from the personal deity. There is no difference

between bliss and emptiness in those powers."
 The key points for this method are:
 One cultivates from a coarse body to the most refined body.
 The illusory body is achieved in this similar way.
 Brilliant light is also achieved this way.
 I often give the example:
 Sunlight,
 Convex mirror, and
 Paper.
 When the sunlight concentrates into a single point on the paper through the convex mirror, "boom," fire is ignited.
 Brilliance is manifested.
 The illusory body is created.
 This is the result of induction!
 I honestly would like to tell everyone that I am not bragging or being boastful!

These postures require oral transmissions and demonstrations, and belong to the method of non-leakage.

Sheng-yen Lu

34. Key Points on Postures for Cultivating One's Body

I would like to tell a joke first:
On a tour bus, a statuesque lady was playing a guessing game. She asked everyone, "Please guess my occupation."
She continued, "Every day, I go to work that requires me to undress. Not only that, I wriggle my waist and shake my buttocks all day long. In addition, I often stretch my legs wide open…"
All the tourists who were listening became embarrassed and quietly thought, "My goodness! What kind of career is that!"
She then revealed that she was a Yoga Instructor.
Ha ha ha!
The posture in some Vajrayana analytic meditation practices is essential. Although it does not require practitioners to do any fist movements, the name of the posture is Vajra Fist.
The first posture: the Seven-featured Meditation Posture
One's tongue touches the upper palate to guide the Heart Qi into the central channel.
One bends the neck down as a hook to guide the Descending Qi

into the central channel. (One's chin presses on the Adam's apple.)

One maintains a straight spine with open shoulders, so that the Circulating Qi can flow into the central channel.

One forms a mudra at the location of the dantian to guide the Balancing Qi to flow into the central channel.

One sits cross-legged to guide the Ascending Qi into the central channel.

One keeps the mouth closed. No speech is allowed.

One stops distracting thoughts and remains focused.

(This is the posture of analytic meditation. It is used frequently.)

The second posture is known as the Six-fire-pit Mudra Sitting Position.

The posture is used for cultivating inner fire. Milarepa was sitting in this posture to successfully accomplish the practice of inner fire.

The practitioner sits with both legs crossed, feet flat on the floor, and both of the upper legs pressed against the navel chakra.

The practitioner embraces the bent legs with the arms crossed.

Throughout this practice, the practitioner must sit upright.

(It is easier to initiate the inner fire by using this method.)

In this posture, pressing on the navel chakra is the key.

The third posture is known as the Vajra Scepter Mudra.

This mudra can be formed in either a standing position or a lying down position.

Both the positions have a similar effect.

The practitioner places his palms together above his head, forming the shape of the upper portion of a vajra scepter.

The practitioner keeps his body straight, similar to the middle portion of a vajra scepter.

The practitioner bends his legs slightly with both soles of the feet touching, similar to the shape of the lower portion of a vajra scepter.

In the standing position, one's toes must touch the ground

supporting one's weight. This makes this position much more difficult. In the lying down position, it is not as difficult to do.

(This mudra transforms the practitioner into a vajra scepter, protecting the practitioner from afflictions and evil obstructions.)

The forth posture is known as the Wrathful Subjugation Mudra.

The practitioner stands and raises his right hand forming the Tarjani Mudra.

The practitioner places his left hand in front of his chest.

The practitioner makes an angry face.

The practitioner stands with his right leg bent and left leg stretching straight out.

(This mudra can subjugate the Four Demons.)

The fifth is a group of three postures for observing light:

The Lion Sitting Posture.

The Lying Elephant Posture.

The Immortal Sitting Posture.

(These three methods require oral transmissions and demonstrations of the postures.)

The sixth type of posture consists of the Mudra of Raising the Light Drops Flying to Mount Sumeru, and The Six Sakya Postures.

These postures require oral transmissions and demonstrations, and belong to the method of non-leakage.

In addition:

The Vajravarahi 27-fist-form Practice and 108-form of Vajra Fist Practice are the practices for guiding qi. The main purpose of the two practices is to assist the circulation of the qi. Guide the qi in the Non-leakage Practice, Inner Fire Practice, and Light Drop Practice with the body mudra.

No one can learn all of them, even in one's life time.

Sheng-yen Lu

35. Key Points on Empowerments

The secret significance of empowerments in Vajrayana Buddhism is the authorization.
Both the method and sequence of receiving empowerments are very important. Vajrayana disciples have to understand the proper method and correct sequence. Do not take them out of order.
Empowerments represent lineage.
Empowerments represent authorization.
Empowerments represent permission.
After becoming a disciple in Vajrayana Buddhism, one should receive empowerments from one's Root Guru, in order to be in accordance with the dharma.
Compared with traditional empowerments, modern ones seem less complex.
In the past, there were steps before receiving an empowerment.
First, one would have to observe the land. Second, one would have to pray to the local earth deity of the land. Third, one would have to purify the land. Fourth, one would have to erect a mandala.
Prior to empowerment, there were six types of rituals to follow:
First, the earth deity ritual. Second, the five objects ritual. Third,

the disciples would have to get prepared. Fourth, bedding would have to be prepared. Fifth, karma threads would have to be prepared. Sixth, auspicious dates would have to be chosen.

The succession of the empowerments were as follows:
The Treasure Vase Empowerments.
The Secret Empowerment.
The Wisdom Empowerment.
The Perfection Empowerment.

The Treasure Vase Empowerments were divided into the Water Empowerment, Personal Deity Empowerment, All Deity Empowerment, Master Empowerment, Dharma Implements Empowerment, Sutra and Tantra Empowerment, Crown Empowerment, Banner Empowerment, Vajra Scepter Empowerment, Vajra Bell Empowerment, Forbidden Empowerment, Title Empowerment, Permission Empowerment, and many more.

The Treasure Vase Empowerments belong to the development stage.

The other three empowerments belong to the completion stage:
The Secret Empowerment. (Internal Practices Empowerment)
The Wisdom Empowerment. (Highest Tantra Empowerment)
The Perfection Empowerment. (The Foremost Empowerment)

I personally feel that the most important key points of empowerments are the following:

Inviting and greeting the wisdom deity.

The wisdom deity descending to the mandala.

Invite the wisdom deity to move from the mandala to the empowerment implement.

Carry out the empowerment for the disciples using the implement.

These procedures are very important.

I remember when I was once in front of the mandala at the Taiwan Lei Tsang Temple. I was intending to transmit the Mahakala empowerment for a disciple.

Mahakala descended from the void.
Mahakala told me, "There is no Mahakala Mandala!"
After confirmation, there was really no Mahakala Mandala, not even a golden statue.
Therefore, Mahakala descended into my body.
I transformed into Mahakala and carried out the empowerment for the disciple. The retinues of Mahakala descended into my body one by one.
(This is a unique situation.)
The implements used for empowerments are as follows:
The Treasure Vase Empowerments – There are many implements.
The Secret Empowerment – Red and white flowers.
The Wisdom Empowerment - A pen.
The Perfection Empowerment – Secret transmission.
I think the meanings in the four levels of empowerments are as follows:
Purification of the karma in one's body.
Purification of the karma in one's speech.
Purification of the karma in one's mind.
The unification of brilliant light and the illusory body.
I have always believed that Vajrayana Buddhism rituals are too numerous and complex. No one can learn all of them, even in one's life time. I have been separating the wheat from the chaff to simplify the rituals as much as possible.
However, the important procedures cannot be omitted.
Remember:
The master must be compassionate.
The disciples must be devout.

In fact, the Buddha-nature is inherently perfect and pure.

Sheng-yen Lu

36. The Hum Syllable Purification Dharma (Speech Dharma)

Following the teachings of our lineage gurus, practitioners can practice the purification dharma of the Hum (ཧཱུྂ) syllable.

The first practice:

From the heart, one silently and continuously chants the "Hum" syllable. (Softly)

Blue Hum syllables are exhaled through the right nostril, one after another.

The Hum syllables permeate one's house, houses in the neighborhood, the sky, land, lakes, oceans, mountains and rivers everywhere.

While chanting continuously, visualize that all the Hum syllables return one by one through the left nostril into one's body.

When the whole body is filled with Hum syllables from head to toe, one shouts "Hum!" The external and the inner worlds are thereby purified.

The second practice:

One chants the Hum syllable vigorously, visualizing a fierce blue-green Hum syllable in the heart.

The violent Hum syllable is released one by one through the left nostril. The fiery, explosive, and thunderous syllables are so powerful like thunder, lightning, and raging fire, that destroy everything in the external world piece by piece with nothing left.

(Through the practice, one realizes that the physical world is without self-nature and reality.)

The blue-green Hum syllables then return to one's body through the right nostril. The practitioner's body is full of vigorous Hum syllables.

With a loud explosion, the practitioner vanishes.

The outside world becomes empty.

The inside world is also empty.

(The practitioner then realizes that neither the outside world nor oneself is real.)

The third practice:

The practitioner visualizes that there is a red Hum syllable outside one's body.

Then the practitioner visualizes their body transforming into a black Hum syllable.

The two Hum syllables grow in size as big as that of Mount Sumeru.

The two Hum syllables approach each other and intertwine.

Then the two Hum syllables become as small as a grain of mustard seed, which fly into one's body through the left and right nostrils, and reside in one's heart.

The practitioner focuses on the red and black Hum syllables.

The practitioner remains peacefully in the state of Samadhi.

(This is a dharma to enter into the state of Samadhi, and abide in gentle meditation)

The fourth practice:

The practitioner's body transforms into a white Hum syllable.

The practitioner's speech transforms into a white Hum syllable.

The practitioner's mind transforms into a white Hum syllable.

With the Hum syllable in the mind, visualize the practitioner walking throughout their house before going outside.

The practitioner walks throughout their own city.

The practitioner walks throughout other cities.

The practitioner walks throughout their own country, the foreign countries, the three realms, the Six Paths and so on.

All filth as long as it is touched by the Hum syllable becomes purified.

All sufferings transform into a Pure Land.

(This is a great purification dharma)

In all the four practices, the practitioner should sit in the Seven-featured Vairocana Posture.

The practitioner should be focused during the practices.

Cultivating the practices will benefit one greatly.

Firstly, one's speech will be purified.

Secondly, one will unite with the Tao.

Thirdly, one will attain the realization that there is no reality.

My key points are:

In fact, the Buddha-nature is inherently perfect and pure. The practices of body, speech and mind all originate from the fundamental self-nature of non-duality.

With this realization, one understands that all practices are within the state of dharma-nature.

The excellent results through these practices are superior.

One who unites with the Tao naturally knows that there is no reality.

Because there is no reality, everything is pure.

The Great Compassion Dharani contains all buddhas, all dharma, and all merits.

Sheng-yen Lu

37. Profound Insight of the Great Compassion Dharani (Speech Dharma)

We understand that Vajrayana Buddhism teaches:
Purifying body with hand and body mudras.
Purifying speech with mantra.
Purifying mind with visualization and no-thoughts.

I hereby would like to discuss the well-known Great Compassion Dharani, a mantra of great merits.

If one often recites the Great Compassion Dharani, one will achieve ten merits in the present life:

First, one will be happy and peaceful. Second, diseases will be eradicated. Third, one will achieve longevity. Fourth, one will be wealthy. Fifth, one's karmic hindrances will be eliminated. Sixth, one will avoid sufferings. Seventh, one will receive great merits. Eighth, one will be fearless. Ninth, one will reach spiritual attainment. Tenth, one will be reborn in the Pure Land.

One will also achieve:

Buddha body, brilliant light, compassion, subtle dharma, meditation, emptiness, fearlessness, eloquence, eternally abiding, liberation, medicine king, and supernatural powers.

The merits are endless.

It also contains five groups of tantric dharmas:

Purification – manifestation of buddha hands and more.

Subjugation – manifestation of the golden wheel hands and more.

Enhancement – manifestation of the wish fulfilling hands and more.

Harmonization – manifestation of the lotus hands and more.

Summoning – manifestation of the precious arrow hands and more.

My profound insight is:

The Great Compassion Dharani contains all buddhas, all dharma, and all merits.

The Great Compassion Dharani is praised by buddhas numerous as the sands of the Ganges.

The Great Compassion Dharani can manifest all the honored ones, esoteric lords, dragon kings, devas, and benevolent deities.

It comprehensively includes all mantras.

It can help one to not only escape from sufferings and attain happiness, but also to raise one's stage of attainment and lotus grade. One will also be reborn in the Pure Land, and attain Buddhahood in the present body.

(I advise everyone to recite the Great Compassion Dharani.)

In addition, I would like to talk about prayer wheels.

Guanyin Bodhisattva gave a prediction to Nagarjuna, "The Dragon King Buddha in the Dragon Palace has a prayer wheel. Anyone who sees, hears, thinks, or touches it, will be freed from the three lower realms. If you obtain the prayer wheel, you will benefit all beings."

Nagarjuna journeyed to the Dragon Palace, and met the Dragon King Buddha. The Buddha said, "This prayer wheel is a gift from Dipamkara Buddha. It has great power, can help beings to escape from sufferings, and can protect all dragons."

Nagarjuna later presented the prayer wheel to Simhamukha, who brought it to Tibet. As a result, all the Tibetan temples have prayer wheels.

The *Karandavyuha Sutra* states, "Turning the prayer wheel results in a great divine power. It eliminates karmic hindrances, and subjugates devils, sickness, natural disasters, imprisonment, wars, and enemies. Turning the prayer wheel once is equal to reciting mantras millions of times. The merits are incredible. Dragon kings, devas and dharma protectors will help to eliminate all the karmic hindrances."

I encourage everyone:

To recite the Great Compassion Dharani.

To practice the Thousand-Armed, Thousand-Eyed Guan Yin Bodhisattva Sadhana.

To turn prayer wheels.

The profound insight I have attained from practicing this dharma is:

My body disappears.

My mind is immovable.

Suppleness.

Dwell openly and widely.

Brilliant light.

Empty-mindedness.

Boundless dharma power.

Holy disciples who understand the short sentences above will surely uncover the secrets of the Thousand-Armed, Thousand-Eyed Guan Yin Bodhisattva and Living Buddha Lian-sheng Sheng-yen Lu.

The key formulas are all contained inside.

Finally contemplating on how one's thoughts disappear and where they go, one will understand that thoughts have nowhere to go.

Sheng-yen Lu

38. Great Wisdom of Brightness and Emptiness (Cultivating one's Mind)

I first would like to explain the key cultivation points in the four levels of Mahamudra:
First, One-Pointedness.
Second, Simplicity.
Third, One Taste.
Fourth, Non-meditation.
What is One-Pointedness?
My answer is:
"There are no thoughts. Since it appears and disappears naturally, even if there is an idea, it is equivalent to having no idea. One is not attached to or confused by anything. There is only emptiness. This is One-Pointedness."
What is Simplicity?
My answer is:
"One does not seize, attach oneself to or rest on any thoughts, but responds to everything naturally and open-mindedly. This is Simplicity."

What is One Taste?
My answer is:
"There is nothing like yours, mine and his, but only equality and non-difference. There are also no so-called achievements or non-achievements. This is One Taste."
What is Nonmeditation?
My answer is:
"There is nothing to pursue. Even if one cultivates, it is equivalent to non-cultivation. Non-cultivation is equal to cultivation. One thoroughly understands the Buddha-nature, and realizes that the Buddha-nature has nothing to do with cultivation or non-cultivation. This is Non-meditation."
(These are important formulas.)
I ask you:
Where are the thoughts coming from?
Where do the thoughts stay?
Where do the thoughts go?
Contemplating firstly on these three questions, one will understand that the mind is free from creation. Then when contemplating on where one's thoughts stay, one will understand that thoughts have no place to stay. Finally contemplating on how one's thoughts disappear and where they go, one will understand that thoughts have nowhere to go.
Therefore:
Thoughts are generated from the emptiness!
Thoughts stay in the emptiness!
Thoughts disappear to the emptiness!
Hence:
"There is no so-called creating, staying, and going. In any case one cannot find the thoughts and the mind."
Since one cannot find the thoughts nor the mind, there is only brightness and emptiness.

I would like to quote a verse by Guru Padmasambhava:
The buddha mind is indeed one's own-nature.
It is constantly in one and there is no need to search.
One who knows this alone is the dharma-body buddha.
This cannot be shown through others.
The major formula for cultivating the mind is:
Don't think that the mind is faulty.
Like the sea and the waves.
Both have the same origin.
There is no right.
There is no wrong.
When reaching this point, there is nothing to talk about anymore.
Everyone should pay attention:
No phenomena.
Mindless.
No self.
Without birth.
I would like to share an anecdote.
A father and son saw a luxurious imported Rolls-Royce.
The son said, "A person who drives that kind of car lacks common sense!"
His father replied lightly, "A person who says that must have no money in their pocket!"
I say, "Everything can be known through logical reasoning!"

If the habitual tendencies of the Six Paths have been completely eliminated, one will have auspicious dreams.

Sheng-yen Lu

39. Eliminating the Habitual Tendencies of the Six Paths

I personally believe and understand that everyone is born with karmic hindrances accumulated from numerous previous lives.

It is because many people are born mentally retarded or physically defective, such as being deaf, mute, missing limbs, low IQ, soft bones, crooked mouths, oblique eyes, large heads, short limbs, and etc.

These people are just born.

They have not committed any good or evil deeds.

Why does this occur?

This is due to the karmic hindrances accumulated from numerous previous lives!

Our habitual tendencies, afflictions, and karmic hindrances are deep-rooted and follow us from our previous lives at birth.

Some are accumulated after being born. They are affected by the surrounding environment, and gradually adopt various habitual tendencies.

We often say:

Dragons give birth to dragons.

Phoenixes give birth to phoenixes.
Mice are born able to dig holes.
Every pickle in the jar tastes the same.
This all results from influence by the surrounding environment after birth.

Following is the key formula for the Vajrayana Buddhism Practice of Eliminating the Habits of the Six Paths:

The practitioner sits in the Seven-featured Vairocana Posture.

The practitioner visualizes the seed syllables corresponding to the Six Paths.

ཨ (Ah), is white in color, and located at the ajna chakra corresponding to the Heavenly Path.

སུ (Su), is green in color, and located at the throat chakra corresponding to the Asura Path.

ནི (Ni), is blue in color, and located at the heart chakra corresponding to the Human Path.

ཞི (Zhi), is red in color, and located at the navel chakra corresponding to the Animal Path.

ཞེ (Zhe), is green in color, and located at the sacral chakra corresponding to the Hungry Ghost Path.

དུ (Du), is a smoky color, and located at the bottom of the feet corresponding to the Hell Path.

(One should remember that all these seed syllables are pale in color.)

The practitioner then visualizes the seed syllables corresponding to the three bodies of a buddha:

(Om), is bright white, and located at the brow chakra.

(Ah), is bright red, and located at the throat chakra.

(Hum), is bright blue, and located at the heart chakra.

When these steps are completed, one proceeds to the following steps.

One visualizes the three buddha syllables beginning to burn. The three syllables emit fire and spread gradually, until the Six-Path seed syllables are all burned and vanish.

The practitioner becomes extremely bright.

The practitioner gently chants "*Om-ah-hum.*"

The practitioner continues the chanting until the six seed syllables are completely burned.

The more one chants "*Om-ah-hum*," the better.

If the habitual tendencies of the Six Paths have been completely eliminated, one will have auspicious dreams.

First, the practitioner flies freely in space.

Second, the practitioner sees his body being transparent as glass.

Third, the practitioner sees white light around his body.

Fourth, the practitioner sees himself wearing white and clean heavenly clothes.

Fifth, the practitioner eats something white and spits out something black.

Sixth, the practitioner takes a shower in white light.

Seventh, the practitioner sees themselves transforming into the personal deity.

At this time, the practitioner will feel that their greed, hatred, ignorance, doubt, arrogance, and jealousy are reduced or disappear.

Internally, the practitioner is peaceful and unhindered.

I personally think that if one has succeeded in the Inner Fire, one may visualize this special syllable " ʂ " burning. (This special syllable is actually an Ah "ཨཱཿ" syllable, in which only the upper left portion is visualized upside down.)

The fire then arises to burn through the body.

Therefore, all the habitual tendencies of the Six Paths are naturally removed, and the practitioner is purified.

I say that the Vajrayana dharma is flexible.

Practitioners can comprehend all dharma through analogies.

One should understand that all the thoughts, which come and go, emerge on their own and vanish on their own.

Sheng-yen Lu

40. The Key Formula for Awareness of Bright Light

Generally, the appearance of bright lights described by a master will include the occurrence of a very short flash of light in daily life. It is difficult to recognize this kind of light. One can only perceive it without any control.

Between the moment when a thought has diminished and the next thought has not yet arisen, the bright light occasionally appears.

Since infants are not disturbed by delusional thoughts, a baby can often see the bright light.

When one is experiencing great bliss, the bright light may suddenly flash.

When one has sneezed, one's mind becomes interrupted and the bright light may flash.

When one yawns, one's mind becomes interrupted and the bright light may flash.

When one is in the state of deep sleep, the bright light may flash.

When one is dying at the bardo state between death and rebirth, the bright light may flash.

When one is knocked unconscious, one's thoughts cease and the bright light may flash.

When one is deeply frightened, one may lose consciousness and the bright light may flash.

Among the appearances of the bright light mentioned above, some are meaningless, some cannot be recognized, and all are difficult to grasp.

We (yogis) remain in the following state:

Non-practice.

Non-remediation.

Non-governing.

Non-scattering.

When the light appears for an extended period of time during meditation, one then is able to be truly aware of the appearance of the bright light.

The following is the key formula for the awareness of the bright light based on my experience:

When thoughts are disordered, let them calm down.

When thoughts are calm, keep them stable.

When thoughts are stable, let them expand.

In this state of expansion, the bright light is born.

(This formula may seem to counteract the various thoughts. In fact, one does not have to counter. One just has to realize that the state of disorder is the mind, calmness is the mind, stability is the mind, the state of expansion is the mind, and the bright light is also the mind. It is both bright and empty.)

One should understand that all the thoughts, which come and go, emerge on their own and vanish on their own.

Metaphorically, I say:

The sea is the Buddha-nature.

The waves are delusional thoughts.

The waves rise and fall.

They always return to the sea of Buddha-nature.
There is no difference between the two.
Metaphorically,
Like a stream flowing continuously
Is the flow of delusional thoughts
Regardless of a linear or winding path
As long as in the natural state
Let it be as is
By abiding in the natural state, yogis will attain absolute enlightenment and brightness.
Clouds, fog and haze, being born in the void, will vanish in the void.
On the condition one verifies the natural state, nothing can hinder oneself.
Subsequently, the purity, freshness, non-hinderance, naturalness, and bright light will appear spontaneously.
There is neither birth nor death.
It is neither dirty nor pure.
There is neither increasing nor decreasing.
No practice, no remediation, no scattering, all abides in nature.
Clearly understand.
When thoughts arise, one should ignore them. Do not follow them.
No matter what thoughts arise, they will naturally vanish.
This is the world of bright light.
No need to do anything. Be non-abiding.
No need to think. Make nothing.
No discrimination and no concentration.
Bright light appears by itself.
Everyone should verify this!

After one attains enlightenment and starts cultivating accordingly, one will be able to see these bright lights.

Sheng-yen Lu

41. The Light of Wisdom

Vajrayana Buddhism believes that each of us has our own inherent Buddha-nature. I believe that the Buddha-nature is "emptiness." This "emptiness" is very difficult to interpret, and can only be characterized as the Light of Wisdom.

Bright light is not an imaginary thing.

Bright light is the true light that emerges after cultivation.

The light of the Buddha-nature is located in one's heart chakra, and is blue in color.

The light of the crown chakra is located at the top of one's head.

The light of the navel chakra is mainly located around one's navel. (It is also hidden in one's heart, throat, and crown chakras.)

The light of the supernatural eyes is located in one's eyes.

(The light connects the eyes to the heart, which is very important. We look inwardly from our eyes. When reaching the highest level in practicing the dharma of looking inwardly, one can see the light of the light drops, the light of connected light drops, and a plane of light. Eventually, one will see bright light shining over one's body. At this time, one has achieved rainbow transformation of Great Rainbow Light Accomplishment.)

These are namely:
Light of light drops,
Vajra chain,
Vajra screen,
Rainbow Transformation.

(If one transmutes the five elements of one's body gradually, element by element, into light, until the flesh is also transformed, one will achieve a rainbow body which represents the light of wisdom.)

Vajrayana Buddhism categorizes the lights as follows:
The light of the physical heart,
The light of the white soft channel,
The light of the far-reaching water,
The pure light of the dharma realm,
The empty light of light drops,
The light of absolute eternal wisdom.

After one attains enlightenment and starts cultivating accordingly, one will be able to see these bright lights.

I personally do not like to memorize those terms, but maintain the awareness of the light. When I meditate under the light awareness, all kinds of lights appear naturally. This is the most important thing.

My key formula is as follows:
Qi enters into the central channel,
The central channel is opened first,
Initiate the inner fire,
Light drops descend,
Light drops are raised,
Water and fire are unified,
Open up the five chakras,
Light appears in the five chakras,
The five chakras transform into light,
The five elements emit light,
The whole body transforms into rainbow light.

(This is the key formula of Sheng-yen Lu. It is also the stages I, Sheng-yen Lu, experienced. Practitioners can use them as a reference when evaluating their own progress; however, my experience may be different from that of other gurus.)

Through practices, I have confirmed the following:

Illuminating phenomenon – I cannot see myself; my inside and outside are transparent, clear, bright, and very pure.

No thoughts – One can see light only without thoughts. One may be able to see light in a very short period of time when the mind is not thoughtless. Only the light that manifests while one has no thoughts will last the longest. This requires deep meditation, reflecting inwardly with the wisdom eye, and to remain open and natural.

Non-abiding – One should not be attached to the light. One should only feel comfortable, indifferent to fame or gain, tranquil, and immeasurably open.

No confusion – One experiences no rebirth, selflessness, no self-nature, and remains in a natural state. At this time, one also enters the state of non-practice, non-rectification, and the state of not being scattered.

At last:

Practicing without practicing.

Be spontaneous and effortless naturally.

There is nobody who is cultivating meditation.

Being enlightened:

Complete non-existence.

In true enlightenment, there are no traces of afflictions, delusions, and desires.

Sheng-yen Lu

42. Guard the Enlightenment Until It Is Solidified

I noticed several practitioners enlightened in theory behave the same as ordinary people. It is equivalent to not being enlightened. Some of them act even worse than unenlightened ones.
 What has happened?
 This occurs because:
 They do not guard their enlightenment.
 They do not solidify their enlightenment.
 Ordinary people are always the slaves to their emotions and desires, whereas the enlightened must not be controlled by their emotions, more importantly not by their desires.
 For example:
 When riding a wild horse (desires), one should tame the horse with an enlightened mind and not allow the farmland to be trampled.
 Also:
 It is like a shepherd herding the sheep. The shepherd calmly tends his flock while the sheep are free to graze.
 Don't let the sheep wander too far.
 Don't let the sheep get lost.
 Don't let the sheep cross the boundary.

Both of the analogies above include being natural but without being scattered.

Being natural: there is nothing to be obtained, nothing to be attached to, nothing matters, be relaxed, and calm.

Not being scattered: be sharp and clear, do not abandon oneself to carelessness, never give up, and handle things with the right moderation.

Because the enlightened understand the absolute truth of human life:

They will not be attached to anything!
They will not be confused!
They will not be afraid of anything!
They will not pursue anything...

The enlightened understand the inherent purity, inherent bright wisdom, and inherent state. The enlightened will naturally abandon their ego, discrimination, and the scattered mind. That is why we see:

True enlightenment.
False enlightenment.
Enlightened in theory.
Enlightened in practice.

In true enlightenment, there are no traces of afflictions, delusions, and desires.

In true enlightenment, one sees the light, purity, no birth, no self, and liberation.

In true enlightenment, one puts aside everything, and abides naturally.

In true enlightenment, greed, anger, ignorance, doubts, and arrogance disappear.

In true enlightenment, one is relaxed, tranquil, and natural.

I remember that Guru Padmasambhava once said:

The heart is like a cloudless sky,
Good and evil karma all disappear,

No way for one to enter the Six Paths,
Bad habits naturally vanish!

Is there reincarnation?
What causes reincarnation?
The truth has not changed nor moved.
There is no life or death.

The self-nature of Tathagatagarbha,
Birth, age, sickness and death are all dismissed and exiled
Purification with no need to be purified,
This is the true buddha.

No reincarnation and no nirvana,
As if being awakened from a dream,
Only the non-dual dharma body remains,
There are no words, nor sounds,
Emptiness, emptiness and emptiness.

One has achieved attainment when one reaches complete unification.

Sheng-yen Lu

43. Key Points for the Three Kinds of Emptiness

Guru Padmasambhava once said:
The external world we see, which is manifested through the feelings of our own heart, is intrinsically empty.

Our physical body is similar. Being a synthesis of the Four Great Elements, its essence is still fundamentally empty.

The consciousness stored inside our physical heart is the Buddha-nature, and the Buddha-nature is also emptiness.

Many manifestations that we see in actuality are totally a play of the mind. The heart is empty, and therefore the essence of the manifestation is empty.

These manifestations are like a play, which will appear and disappear. They are still fundamentally empty.

I say, "Empty, empty, empty, empty, empty."

There is a yoga of three kinds of emptiness in Vajrayana Buddhism. Its key points are as follows:

One chooses an elevated place to perform the practice, such as a mountain top, the top of a skyscraper, a balcony, or any place that is elevated and quiet, without interference from people walking by.

One should sit in either the immortal sitting posture or the Seven-featured Meditation Posture.

One should practice the yoga on a sunny, cloudless day that is not windy.

The cultivation procedure is as follows:

While staring at the cloudless, clear sky, one unifies oneself with the cloudless, clear, wide and spacious sky.

The sky is me.

I am the sky.

One becomes the void.

One then looks inwardly to observe one's own light of absolute eternal wisdom, which becomes illuminating.

The absolute eternal wisdom light of Buddha-nature reaches directly to one's eyes through the Crystal Channel.

There is also soft white light inside the Crystal Channel.

Then, the external light, light inside the channel, and the absolute eternal wisdom light unify together. One then enters into the bright meditation of the three kinds of emptiness.

At this time, one becomes like a drop of water merging into the sea. This is also the unification of the child light with the mother light.

In a state of non-meditation, non-rectification, and non-scattering, one gradually increases one's own light. One has achieved attainment when one reaches complete unification.

There are conditions to practice this yoga:

Firstly, the practitioner has opened his heart chakra, and witnessed the absolute eternal wisdom light of the Buddha-nature.

Secondly, the practitioner has witnessed the light of his own channels, the central channel, the three main channels and all the channels of the body including even the Crystal Channel.

Thirdly, only at this time, the unification of external light, the channel lights, and the absolute eternal wisdom light can be realized.

Through the unification of the three lights, the practitioner enters into meditation, and achieves the union of the child light with the mother light.

(The external light referred to here can be regarded as the cosmic consciousness.)

I would like to tell a joke:

A young man asked a Zen master, "I can't let something go."

The Zen master threw a piece of pork belly which he was about to place in his mouth into the trash.

The young man asked, "Are you suggesting that I should not eat meat, become a vegetarian and achieve Buddhahood instantly?"

The Zen master replied, "I want to tell you that people are pork bellies. They should throw themselves away."

(Ha ha ha!)

Speaking in another way, the Buddha-nature is at the center, and is surrounded by a group of brilliant light drops.

Sheng-yen Lu

44. Key Formulas to Witness the Buddha-nature

I believe that in order to witness the Buddha-nature, there are four sitting postures:
First, the Seven-featured Vairocana Posture.
Second, the lion posture.
Third, the elephant posture.
Fourth, the immortal posture.
(These are the key formulas related to one's physical body.)
The key formula related to the speech is:
Keep silent,
Remain mute.
The key formulas related to the mind are:
Not to be scattered,
No practice,
No remediation,
Not to be distinctive, but remain open, relaxed, natural, non-abiding.
The formulas to observe light are:
In the lion posture, one observes the moonlight by looking up with one's two eyes.

In the immortal posture, one observes electric lights by looking down at the lights.

In the elephant posture, one observes the sunlight at noon by looking at the light peripherally.

In the Seven-featured Vairocana Posture, one observes one's inner light.

There are six kinds of light:

Light of the heart.
Light of the channels.
Light of the water.
Light of the dharma realm.
Light of the light drops.
Light of the absolute eternal wisdom.

(The light of the heart is the light of the absolute eternal wisdom, which manifests within the light of the dharma realm, through the lights of the channels and water.)

This is the attainment of the Buddha-nature!

In addition, there are points of light around the light of the absolute eternal wisdom, which are the lights of the light drops.

Speaking in another way, the Buddha-nature is at the center, and is surrounded by a group of brilliant light drops.

These light drops connect together and form a vajra chain.

Many vajra chains coalesce and form a vajra screen.

All buddhas appear on the vajra screen.

The illusory bodies of all buddhas unify with the light of the absolute eternal wisdom.

This is attainment of Buddhahood.

The cultivation process is as follows:

First one sees the lights of the light drops. Then one opens the light of the heart. While the feeling grows, the vajra chain appears, followed by the appearance of the vajra screen. Then all the buddhas and their pure lands emerge filling the void.

The practitioner transmutes the five elements into a rainbow, and the two unify into one.

This is the rainbow transformation body.

In addition, my personal experience is as follows:

When a practitioner sees the vajra screen and all buddhas and pure lands appearing on the screen, the practitioner then needs to transport their own light of absolute eternal wisdom (Buddha-nature) from the crown chakra, using the qi. The practitioner's Buddha-nature merges into the sea of bright light filling the void.

This is the unification of the mother light with the child light.

In addition:

When a practitioner is dying, the bardo body emerges. Swiftly, the practitioner sees an ocean of bright light.

The practitioner should cast the light from the bardo body into the sea of the bright light and unify the two into one.

This is attainment of Buddhahood from the bardo state.

In addition:

When a practitioner is dying, the bardo body emerges and may see Amitabha Buddha, Avalokitesvara Bodhisattva and Mahasthamaprapta Bodhisattva coming to welcome them.

The practitioner's bardo body should follow and leave.

This is attainment of Buddhahood through guidance.

The key moment occurs when unification takes place.

Things like school, love, career, wealth, longevity, children, beauty and many more are all dreams and illusions.

Sheng-yen Lu

45. The Ultimate Key Points of Sheng-yen Lu (Part 1)

Dear Holy Disciples:
One should practice the rituals of Vajrayana Buddhism and follow the true meanings of the key points in the teachings. The former is about practicing diligently and the latter is about solidifying the state of awakening.

It is important to remember that the teachings we have learned for our worldly obligations are expediency, which will not last long and has no self-nature. All is an illusion.

All worldly obligations are within the cycle of reincarnation. No matter which path one occupies in the Realm of Heavens, Asuras, Humans, Hells, Animals, or Hungry Ghosts, one completely lacks non-hinderance.

Therefore, the teachings through our worldly obligations can be referred to as "guidance," "elementary," "temporary" and "expediency."

Here are a few examples of those teachings:

Be a good person.

Do kind things.

Transform the ten evil deeds into the ten moral deeds. (evil antidote)

(This is the common vehicle of all religions)

These are all illusory acts conducted within an illusion. They are also the illusory phenomena of reincarnation that is based on the Law of Cause and Effect.

The true ultimate key point is to attain enlightenment:

"Life is a big dream."

"Life is a drama."

"Life is reincarnation."

"Life is emptiness."

"Life gains nothing."

"Life has nothing to abide in."

One should awaken from this life, and remain in the state of clear awakening. Completely awakened can be considered as slightly enlightened.

Things like school, love, career, wealth, longevity, children, beauty and many more are all dreams and illusions.

Everything obtainable through effort is temporary. Even if one is rich for many life times, the wealth will disappear eventually.

Even if one has longevity, one will die eventually.

Even if one has the highest rank, one will lose it eventually.

Even if one has true love, it is just a beautiful dream.

Even if one has lots of money, it is only temporary.

Everything is empty.

Nothing is to be gained.

There is no non-hinderance.

My ultimate key point is:

Reincarnation is inevitable; hence, do not reject it; causality is inevitable; do not reject it as well.

We should proceed without interfering in the illusory phenomenon of reincarnation that is based on the Law of Cause and Effect. However, at the same time, we should maintain a state of awakening, gradually accept the ultimate teachings and key points of Living Buddha Lian-sheng Sheng-yen Lu, and take the path of meditation.

Maintaining the awakened state in meditation is most precious.

Each and every effort in the world has never brought about non-hinderance.

Instead:

Awakening will result in non-hinderance.

One can attain non-hinderance through enlightenment, proceeding without interfering, strengthening the state of awakening, openness and relaxation.

There is no peace and happiness if one is in pursuit.

There will be peace and happiness without pursuit.

There is no peace and happiness if one is attached.

There will be peace and happiness without attachment.

Do you understand?

My awakening does not need to be proven, because only the Buddha can truly validate.

Sheng-yen Lu

46. The Ultimate Key Points of Sheng-yen Lu (Part 2)

Dear Holy Disciples:
When I harboured thoughts of revulsion towards this world, I began to seek liberation through Christianity, Taoism, Sutrayana Buddhism, Vajrayana Buddhism, and other paths.

A devout heart rose within me that was very steadfast. I wanted to find the truth, practice the truth, until I became the truth.

I looked for masters and gurus, and began studying the teachings in many sutras and tantras.

My masters taught me.

The sacred books gave me teachings.

After contemplating for three decades, I finally understood and became enlightened.

THIS is it!

What is THIS?

I honestly would like to tell everyone:

THIS is inherently present.

THIS has perpetually existed.

THIS has no discriminating thought.
THIS cannot be obtained from praying.
THIS cannot be obtained from blessings.
THIS cannot be obtained from practices.
THIS can neither be obtained from the stage of insight, cultivation, act, and fruition.
It turns out that Buddhadharma is expediency.
It turns out that Buddhadharma is a tool.
One can use this tool to remove obstacles layer by layer.
After all obstacles are removed, one can find that THIS is right here.
The Buddhadharma is not THIS.
THIS is not the Buddhadharma.
There is no relationship between the two at all.
In Hinayana Buddhism:
Sarvastivada is a tool.
Sautrantika is also a tool.
In Mahayana Buddhism:
Consciousness is a tool. (Asanga Bodhisattva)
The Middle Way is a tool. (Nagarjuna Bodhisattva)
Rangtong, Shetong, Svatantrika, and Prasangika are also just tools.
All this time, these tools have accompanied and assisted me in opening treasure doors one by one.
Finally, I discovered THIS.
Thus, Shakyamuni Buddha once said:
"All Buddhadharma must be abandoned, not to mention non-Buddhadharma!"
My awakening does not need to be proven, because only the Buddha can truly validate.
My awakening also does not need to be rejected nor expelled, because THIS is naturally so. The self-nature does not rely on conditions, nor attach to anything. Even if the self-nature abides, in

truth there is no-abiding.

THIS is not "to be" something.

THIS is not "not to be" something.

Since I have awakened THIS, I have spread the Buddhadharma throughout this human world, using my pure and bright mind which is persistent and everywhere, away from all thoughts and affectation. I live a life in the state of being natural, not greedy, not angry, not ignorant, not doubtful, and not arrogant.

However, I am still continuously bringing forth my expanded and compassionate bodhicitta for the benefit of sentient beings.

I sympathize with the sentient beings who have not found THIS yet. I endeavor to make sentient beings happy without being attached to the result.

This is just a wish!

This wish is also empty!

I clearly understand that it is rarely achievable!

But I still persist with non-hinderance!

Since attaining enlightenment, I have undertaken the mission naturally without attachment to anything.

Only Emptiness, Dharma Nature, and Reality are immutable and permanent.

Sheng-yen Lu

47. The Ultimate Key Points of Sheng-yen Lu (Part 3)

Dear Holy Disciples:

We truly must receive the four levels of empowerments.

The four levels of empowerments are:

First, the Treasure Vase Empowerments – The Five Aggregates are the Five Dhyani Buddhas.

Second, Secret Empowerment – Mantra, qi, channels, and light drops.

Third, Highest Yoga Tantra Empowerment – Emptiness in great bliss (bliss and emptiness are the same.)

Fourth, the Great Perfection Empowerment - complete enlightenment of true wisdom.

The gurus who I have received empowerments from are His Holiness the 16th Karmapa, Guru Sakya Zheng-kong, also known as H.E. Dezhung Rinpoche, Reverend Liao Ming, and Guru Thubten Dargye.

The locations where I have received the empowerments are Upstate New York, Seattle Sakya Monastery in the USA, Jiji Great Mountain in Taiwan, and Ching Yum Fat Kok in Hong Kong.

My most important ultimate key points are:

I have witnessed the Reality, which is also called Thusness. This cannot be explained in languages or words, because it goes beyond all concepts.

But I can explain it expediently as follows:

It is unity, absolute, dharma nature, emptiness, exists constantly, has no differentiation, and everyone possesses it.

I often use empty space to characterize it, or use "this," "so and so," "this is it," and "naturally so."

Dharma nature and emptiness are present permanently, not different, and inherent in everyone.

It is not gained through practicing, because it exists naturally.

Tibetan gurus prefer to use the following analogy:

Taking honey as an example, we can describe it, analyze it, and depict it, so that everyone has a concept of honey. However, it will never be as good as tasting it, and savoring it yourself.

It is the same for the dharma nature and Thusness. You have to personally see, personally listen, personally taste, and personally experience it in order to clearly understand it.

I often use empty space for the interpretation of ultimate truth. Everything is like the moon in water, or a flower in a mirror. Dharma nature and Thusness is originally like empty space, and a cloudless sky.

Since the primordial beginning, it has been empty.

Afflictions and habitual tendencies are like clouds or fog in the empty space.

One uses the Buddhadharma as a tool to remove them.

The empty space will then appear.

The eighty-four thousand dharmas are also tools. All dharmas are tools to remove afflictions, habitual tendencies, and karmic hindrances. All dharmas are flexible, not immutable, and not the goal.

One should know that there is only one thing which is immutable throughout the universe. This immutable thing is referred to as dharma nature, Thusness, Emptiness, and Reality.

All other things are a combined form. What is a combined form? Shakyamuni Buddha said that a person is a combined form of the earth, water, fire, wind, and emptiness. A house is a combined form of wood, stone, metal, water and glass. A car is a combined form of metal, plastics, and machinery.

Everything in the material world is in a combined form.

All combined forms have no self-nature.

Only Emptiness, Dharma Nature, and Reality are immutable and permanent.

For example, people's bodies and minds will change, as they are impermanent.

These must be experienced.

We achieve awakening and enlightenment from these experiences!

Only the crystal sword of supreme wisdom can cut down the tree of egocentrism.

Sheng-yen Lu

48. The Ultimate Key Points of Sheng-yen Lu (Part 4)

Dear Holy Disciples:
My gurus have told me before:
Prior to reaching the secret territory of highest achievement, there is a river of rapids that one must cross. The water flowing in the river lacks buoyancy, therefore it cannot support anything, not even a feather. Therefore nobody can cross.

There is a giant tree beside the river. The height of this tree is the width of the river.

No sword or axe is able to cut the tree. If one could cut down the tree and lay it across the river, one could cross over.

However if one has a sword made of crystal, one could cut down the giant tree.

With the giant tree lying across the river, one can now reach the secret land of highest achievement.

The tree, the river and the sword are symbolic metaphors.

The river that nobody can cross represents reincarnation.

The giant tree represents attachment to self.

The crystal sword represents wisdom.

The meaning of the metaphor is since a common sword or axe absolutely cannot cut down the tree of egocentrism of worldly people, the average person cannot cross the river of reincarnation.

Only the crystal sword of supreme wisdom can cut down the tree of egocentrism.

The sword of supreme wisdom (crystal sword) symbolizes the purity of the realization of the emptiness, which is pure as a crystal.

I would like to say:

The purity of the realization of the emptiness is the awakening mind. The awakening mind is enlightenment.

In Zen, enlightenment analogies are used:

First, a tower without openings.

Second, a guitar without strings.

Third, a bucket painted completely black.

Fourth, a tree without roots.

Fifth, a person dragging their own dead body.

And many more.

I realized:

Rangtong is a special religious sect which points out "the essence of the emptiness of all dharmas." This differentiates itself from "treating everything as real." Believing everything is real is attachment.

Shetong is a religious sect which particularly points out the nature of bright light and Buddha-nature, so practitioners do not fall into complete emptiness of stubborn emptiness.

My key points are:

Rangtong is the essence of the Buddha-nature, whereas Shetong is the function of the Buddha-nature. Such, such. Thus, thus, and so forth

The former is the Middle Way.

The latter is the Doctrine of Consciousness-only.

I would like to tell my disciples that the experience of realization through my own mind is simply wonderful. Surprisingly, I now have no attachment nor fear at all.

I would like to tell everyone that our home, character, life, environment, time, space, actions, thoughts and much more are constantly changing. They cannot last forever.

However, the dharma nature or thusness is eternal.

From this, one should know:

There is no conception of self.

There is no conception of person.

There is no conception of being.

There is no conception of lifespan.

The ultimate important key for us in cultivating Vajrayana Buddhism is enlightenment, or seeking the Buddha-nature. The paths of practices vary, but the sacred land that practitioners arrive at is the same. The unchangeable is emptiness, and full awareness.

One must be free of confusions, act unconditionally, and arrive at a state of balance and stability.

Sheng-yen Lu

49. The Ultimate Key Points of Sheng-yen Lu (Part 5)

Dear Holy Disciples:
All the key points in this book are symbolic.
There are still key points within the key points.
I would like to tell everyone:
The key points are expedient skills. When a practitioner is mature and ready, a clue could assist them to become enlightened.
The following are examples:
Deshan Blow - Zen Master Deshan was famous for using a staff to give his disciples a blow to the head.
Rinzai Shout - Zen Master Rinzai would suddenly shout at his disciples.
Venerable Tilopa transmitted his key point to Venerable Naropa by slapping him in the face using one of his slippers.
In order to persuade the Elephant God Ganesh, Avalokitesvara Bodhisattva embraced him.
I converted a disciple through a dream. In the disciple's dream, I delivered his deceased ancestors to heaven by dancing with them.

Sometimes, through my blessing, the blind can see, the deaf can hear, the mute can speak, and the crippled can walk.

My purpose for doing this is to fulfill the Samaya precepts. Another purpose is for disciples to recognize their own awareness of brightness, and unify their minds with the dharma nature. However, in order to spread the Buddhadharma and enlighten sentient beings, I still have to utilize a variety of expedient methods and supernatural manifestations.

Specifically speaking:

Our physical bodies are constantly changing, and will not last long. Even our minds change and do not last forever.

The only permanent existence is the dharma body.

I would like to tell everyone:

We practitioners should keep our minds pure and bright, avoiding confusion. One must be free of confusions, act unconditionally, and arrive at a state of balance and stability. This is also the basic skill to enter Samadhi, a state of complete equanimity.

Although the ultimate key points I have written so far are essentially important and the primary intent is to enlighten everyone that self-nature is namely the emptiness, it will probably continue to be a secret for ordinary sentient beings. One with sharper capacity may potentially well perceive the key points of this level.

I say that quiescent mind is the Buddha Jewel Sambodhi.

Meditation with non-meditation is the Dharma Jewel.

"I" represents the totality of the Sangha Jewel. However, "I" is a concept, not the self.

This "I" represents nature.

Seriously speaking:

There are no studies, cultivation methods, meditations, nor key points to realize the ultimate truth. Who can understand complete non-existence?

My key points are:

Freedom.
Liberation.
Ha, ha, ha.

The dharma body is my foremost truth! It does not rely on any methods, and it is naturally perfect and pure.

The dharma body is absolute and non-dual. Therefore, there is neither good nor evil.

The dharma body is always the highest and peaceful. I would like to use empty space to characterize this state, although it is not even a state.

It surpasses everything.

It is achievement of non-achievement.

It has neither inside nor outside.

Attainment and non-attainment are also an illusion.

If a practitioner comes to consult me for the true key point of enlightenment, I would respond:

Be peaceful and happy!

There is no differentiation in the dharma nature!

The dharma body is equal!

50. A Letter from Master Lianhe

To the most respected Root Guru, Living Buddha Lian-sheng, How are you!

In a few days I will fly to Taiwan. Although the journey is long, and will take more than thirty hours to fly, the thought of being able to see Grandmaster touches my heart! Since being elected to the Core Committee of the True Buddha Foundation (TBF), I have been able to see Grandmaster each time I attend a core committee meeting. I still become excited every time I meet Grandmaster regardless of the frequency. Upon seeing Grandmaster, I am constantly attracted by Grandmaster's compassionate eyes, bright smiles and the illuminating brilliance of Grandmaster's body. My eyes simply cannot move away from Grandmaster. A friend of mine commented that how come I don't see anyone else the moment I lay my eyes on Grandmaster. Ha, Ha! It is something I cannot control! This happens because Grandmaster's charisma is so strong!

In the hope of spending the Chinese New Year with Grandmaster, I purposely planned to fly to Taiwan before the Chinese Lunar New Year. I wonder if indeed I will see Grandmaster on the Eve of Chinese New Year? I once spent New Year's Day 2000 with Grandmaster. As it was the year before a new millennium, the reunion symbolized a tie between a root guru and his disciple over a millennium. However, I have never spent a Chinese New Year's Day or Eve with Grandmaster. I have also never had the chance to personally wish Grandmaster a happy Chinese New Year and accept a blessed red envelope from Grandmaster! Therefore, this year I made a special request to my brother in Shanghai to take care of my mother in Brazil. This will allow me to fly to Taiwan to spend the Chinese New Year with Grandmaster! How joyful this moment will be! What can be more meaningful and happier than spending the Chinese New Year's Day with one's spiritual mentor and teacher of life!

Some time ago during a dharma speech, Grandmaster mentioned about entering into a retreat. My heart became deeply saddened. As a disciple, I well understand the impermanence taught by the Buddha, and in truth, there is no birth. I also understand that a buddha like Grandmaster has never come nor gone. Sentient beings and I are all illusions, or even no illusions. Nevertheless, my heart was so seriously in pain that not even emptiness can resolve the matter. This connection between a guru and his disciple neither can be cut off by life or death. The love of a guru and his disciple will not be abandoned even after attaining Buddhahood!

Every two months, I have to fly halfway around the Earth for twenty to thirty hours in order to attend a TBF Core Committee meeting. Honestly, the lengthy travel is most difficult. However, everything becomes worthwhile and all the hardships vanish when I am preoccupied by the thought of being able to see Grandmaster shortly.

Therefore, we pray for our Root Guru not to give up on his disciples. Without you, we are a group of helpless, lonely disciples. We are a group of disciples whose lives have become meaningful because of you. We are a group of disciples who consider you as their faith in life. It can be said that we are a group of disciples who were born because of you, and you are the Root Guru who was born because of us! We are the cause of existence of life for one another!

Dear Grandmaster, as your disciple, I have been diligent and vigorous in my dharma practices. I am trying to do my best! I have always felt that diligently practicing the secret formulas as taught by a root guru is the greatest respect and the greatest offering to the root guru. Therefore, no matter how busy I am, whether it is in bringing my mother to the hospital, sleeping in her operating room, or accompanying her in rehabilitation, as long as I have time, I will immediately sit down and commence concentration on the completion of the homework you assigned.

Speaking of my mother, during this period, not only has she received knee replacement surgery, but also her lungs, eyes, ears, and heart all require medical treatment. We visited the hospital forty-two times just for her knee rehabilitation, not to mention many other treatments. However, no matter how busy I am, even during long visitations in the hospital, as long as I have a little time, I'll immediately chant the mantras, enter into meditation, and practice inner fire. Despite the fact that I was very exhausted and busy during this period of time, I completed my daily homework including four times of the Kalachakra and Inner Fire Practices, as well as various qi practices and more. It truly felt like I was racing against time during this period.

Regarding the Kalachakra Dharma, I am practicing the Meditation of One Taste, the key formula taught by you. After unifying with Kalachakra, I visualize that blue light is shining brightly in my heart chakra. My form, sensation, conceptions, volitions, and consciousness are transformed into emptiness. My body becomes an empty shell. Even all my thoughts and awareness disappear. There is only the blue light from my heart shining everywhere inside my body. Then I visualize the blue light shining outside of my body, towards all sentient beings that have an affinity. The form, sensation, conceptions, volitions, and consciousness of all sentient beings dissolve and disappear in the blue light. As a result, all sentient beings transform into the Kalachakra Buddha emitting illustrious blue light. We are completely uniform, integrating with each other into a sea of blue light. This is the ocean of True Suchness and Buddha-nature…

As for the Inner Fire Practice, your recent discourses on the key formulas of inner fire have been an immense help. Now the inner fire inside my body is no longer a large area of heat, but a concentrated bright light beam, which rises along the central channel. While passing through the heart chakra, the light beam is like a light pillar that is passing through a centre axle, enhancing the strength of the light existing in the heart chakra. When the light beam reaches my brain, my whole brain illuminates, as if it has melted into a bright ocean of light. In the final stage of entering into the Inner Fire Samadhi, the internal scene I experienced was very similar to what we have observed above the Ling Shen Ching Tze Temple on the birthday of Ksitigarbha Bodhisattva. I observed endless lights in my crown chakra, my personal deity shining brightly in my heart chakra, and millions of light rays shining into the sky from below. The scene was wonderful and beyond words. This is all thanks to the subtle formulas within your teachings, and your blessings!

As for the Sword Tempering and Non-leakage Methods, I have made great progress since our last consultation in Seattle. Now I practice the Sword Tempering Method every day. First I'll let the light drops descend, and then I'll reverse the flow of light drops instantly and forcefully by contracting my limbs with the whole body fiercely and strongly. The rising of light drops is complete and swift, which gives me the feeling of being a real powerful yogi.

Thanks for your very precious teachings and blessings. I often see you in my dreams, and receive blessings from you. I remember one day I hurt my back while playing ball with some dharma brothers. The injury caused great pain in my cervical spine. Also during this period of time, while giving blessings to a dharma brother who was seriously ill, I was affected by his yin qi. As a result, I could not fall asleep at night due to the soreness and pain I felt. It turned out when I was half-asleep, you appeared. While you were holding my head, your head touched mine. Your hand gently stroked my head as if you were helping a child to fall asleep. In this way, I gradually fell asleep. After waking up, my whole body felt relaxed, all the soreness and yin qi were gone, and everything became bright and auspicious again! Grandmaster, your blessing is so far-reaching. It is so effortless for you to reach me even if we are tens of thousands of miles apart. This is most incredible!

Dear Grandmaster, during the recent New Year holiday period, about 50 disciples from Zhendi Lei Tseng Temple in Brazil went to a beach with me and practiced vigorously. We rented a beach house located at the top of a mountain not far from the sea. The scenery was extremely beautiful with the surrounding green trees and ocean view. While staying there, we cultivated for seven days and six nights continuously. We practiced four times daily, focusing on the White Maha Padmakumara Yoga.

Every day, I lead the group to practice the visualization of the White Maha Padmakumara, dignified in appearance wearing fluttering celestial garments. Then we recited the heart mantra together, experiencing the blessings and intense light of the White Maha Padmakumara. We then practiced the Nine Cycle Breathing Exercise, breathing as though we were one with you. Since you recently have emphasized the importance of the Nine Cycle Breathing Exercise, we practiced not just one time, but three times, with a total of twenty-seven inhalations and exhalations. This allowed everyone to feel the warmth of the buddha light flowing into the three channels of one's body. This also allowed everyone to gradually become calm through breathing subtly, slowly and at great length.

We all then entered meditation together, visualizing the White Maha Padmakumara shining and sitting on one's crown. Then the White

Maha Padmakumara descended down to one's brain and emitted light, down to one's throat chakra and emitted light, and then down to one's heart chakra and emitted light. Everyone's internal body was illuminated as bright as daylight by the White Maha Padmakumara's expansive light, expelling the darkness inside everyone's heart.

Finally, everyone unified with the White Maha Padmakumara. All present transformed into the White Maha Padmakumara. This was a great assembly of countless Padmakumaras. All the Padmakumaras shone upon each other. The whole villa and the entire beach were transformed into a beautiful Pure Land of Maha Twin Lotus Ponds......

We all felt exaltation and enjoyed greatly this kind of diligent group cultivation! Everyone made progress in the quality of their meditation. Some disciples even saw that everyone was emitting light during the meditation. We were all full of dharma joy, and extremely happy! Since the extensive cultivation, everyone has felt that our visualization of the White Maha Padmakumara has been very easy and clear. Later, when we returned to the Lei Teng Temple at San Paulo, during the fire offering ceremony, the dharma flow of the whole ceremony was very strong, moving, and astonishing!

During this period we also practiced the Dragon Treasure Vase Dharma seven times. At the same time we prayed for an auspicious New Year for all disciples in 2014, we also specially prepared a large treasure vase, which was filled with herbs and precious stones, along with the precious materials blessed by Grandmaster. This big vase was specially designed to wish for a True Buddha compound to be established in Brazil! We hope that we can locate some precious land which has excellent feng shui and is suitable for cultivation. Thus we will be able to purchase the land and construct the True Buddha compound and a huge buddha statue.

There were auspicious signs when we were cultivating at the seaside. A rainbow appeared continuously near the villa for several days. The magnificent rainbow rose from the sea to the mountain, forming a complete arch. Not only one but two beautiful rainbows appeared directly in front of us. This spectacular scene was moving and blissful. On the last day, while we went to the sea and made vase offerings to the Dragon King, the sky was blue with sunshine. However, the moment we returned to the villa, suddenly thunder boomed, lightning flashed, and rain poured until midnight. The thunderstorm eliminated days of drought!

After these seven days and six nights of diligent cultivation, everyone felt very good about living and practicing together! We all yearn for such a life, looking forward to the future when the True Buddha compound will soon be built. Then we can be together every day, practicing four times daily, practicing qi and yoga daily, and exercising and singing every day! Everyone is very happy together because we have a common belief, common Buddhadharma, common Root Guru, common mantras, common visualizations and a common dream of achieving realization together! Therefore, we pray for your blessing of securing a large plot of land with auspicious geomancy as soon as possible. We pray for your entering into our dreams, guiding us to find such a precious area of land which can assist everyone to attain realization and save sentient beings!

We all want to learn from Ksitigarbha Bodhisattva, and follow the way of Monk Kim Gyo-gak of Jiuhua Mountain who lived and practiced together with a group of like-minded practitioners. As a result, many practitioners achieved Buddhahood in their present body. Many of these practitioners had left behind their own whole-body relics for modern people to admire. We pray for the True Buddha compound to become our treasure land where we will practice, live, and achieve Buddhahood together in the future! We pray single-mindedly for your blessings!

Beloved Grandmaster, the year of 2014, a year of the heavenly steed soaring across the sky, has arrived; I sincerely wish you and Shi Mu:

Happy New Year! Peace and good health! May you smile every

day, and may each and every day be auspicious! May you effortlessly transmit the True Buddha Tantric Dharma! May all True Buddha disciples achieve attainment! I also pray for you to indicate the areas where I should focus attention regarding my practices in the new year. I pray for you to bless me to be successful in my dharma practices during this Year of the Horse. I pray for perfect achievement in my Kalachakra, inner fire, non-leakage, and light drop practices so that I will attain the Buddhahood in the present body, transform into rainbow light, and benefit numerous sentient beings in the future!

I hereby thank and pay sincere homage to Grandmaster!

Your humble disciple, Lianhe
January 17, 2014
San Paulo, Brazil
PS: Shortly after, I listened to Grandmaster's discourse on the key formula of the Great Perfection:

Spreading the "Hum" syllables covering mountains, rivers, and all the dharma realms. My heart was exceptionally filled with joy!

Thank you so much, Grandmaster!

Also From US Daden Culture

Sheng-yen Lu Book Collection 51:
Highest Yoga Tantra and Mahamudra

Sale Price: $12.00 USD
ISBN: 978-0-9841561-6-0

Sheng-yen Lu Book Collection 129:
Entering the Most Hidden Yin-Yang Realm

Sale Price: $12.00 USD
ISBN: 978-0-9960699-1-5

Sheng-yen Lu Book Collection 148:
The Power of Mantra

Sale Price: $12.00 USD
ISBN: 978-0-9841561-1-5

Sheng-yen Lu Book Collection 154:
The Aura of Wisdom

Sale Price: $12.00 USD
ISBN: 978-0-9841561-4-6

US DADEN

3440 Foothill Blvd. • Oakland, CA 94601 • U.S.A. • www.usdaden.c

Also From US Daden Culture

Sheng-yen Lu Book Collection 158:
Contemplation Under the Lonesome Light

Sale Price: $12.00 USD
ISBN: 978-0-9960699-9-1

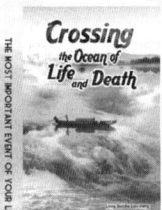

Sheng-yen Lu Book Collection 163:
Crossing the Ocean of Life and Death

Sale Price: $12.00 USD
ISBN: 978-0-9841561-0-0

Sheng-yen Lu Book Collection 166:
Travel to Worlds Beyond
Sale Price: $12.00 USD

ISBN: 978-0-9841561-2-2
Ebook available

Sheng-yen Lu Book Collection 200:
Pages and Pages of Enlightenment
Sale Price: $12.00 USD
ISBN: 978-0-9841561-5-3
Ebook available

3440 Foothill Blvd. • Oakland, CA 94601 • U.S.A. • www.usdaden.com

Also From US Daden Culture

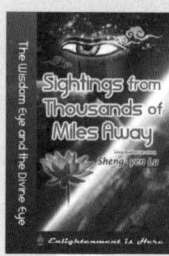

Sheng-yen Lu Book Collection 202:
Sightings from Thousands of Miles Away

Sale Price: $12.00 USD
ISBN: 978-0-9841561-3-9

Sheng-yen Lu Book Collection 204:
The Divine Book

Sale Price: $12.00 USD
ISBN: 978-0-9960699-0-8

Sheng-yen Lu Book Collection 218:
Remembrance of the Moon River

Sale Price: $12.00 USD
ISBN: 978-0-9858080-6-8

Sheng-yen Lu Book Collection 220:
Q&A with A Contemporary Dharma King, Vol. 2

Sale Price: $12.00 USD
ISBN: 978-0-9963807-2-0

Sold at amazon.com or at www.tbboyeh.org/eng#/

Also From US Daden Culture

Sheng-yen Lu Book Collection 223:
Stories of Supreme Spiritual Responses

Sale Price: $12.00 USD
ISBN: 978-0-9858080-5-1

Sheng-yen Lu Book Collection 226:
Open Your Mind

Sale Price: $12.00 USD
ISBN: 978-0-9963807-4-4

Sheng-yen Lu Book Collection 236:
The Magical Hands of Sheng-yen Lu

Sale Price: $12.00 USD
ISBN: 978-0-9963807-0-6

Sheng-yen Lu Book Collection 238:
Intimate Talk with the Moon

Sale Price: $12.00 USD
ISBN: 978-0-9963807-1-3

3440 Foothill Blvd. • Oakland, CA 94601 • U.S.A. • www.usdaden.com

Also From US Daden Culture

Sheng-yen Lu Book Collection 240:
Gateway to Infinite Dharma Treasure

Sale Price: $12.00 USD
ISBN: 978-0-9963807-5-1

Sheng-yen Lu Book Collection 246:
Chatting with Oneself

Sale Price: $12.00 USD
ISBN: 978-0-9963807-3-7

Sheng-yen Lu Book Collection 254:
The Most Glorious Realization

Sale Price: $12.00 USD
ISBN: 978-0-9963807-7-5

Sheng-yen Lu Book Collection 196:
Refreshing Messages

Sale Price: $12.00 USD
ISBN: 978-0-9963807-6-8

Sold at amazon.com or at www.tbboyeh.org/eng#/